Second Edition

IN THE FIELD

A GUIDE FOR THE SOCIAL WORK PRACTICUM

William A. Danowski

Boston   Columbus   Indianapolis   New York   San Francisco   Upper Saddle River
Amsterdam   Cape Town   Dubai   London   Madrid   Milan   Munich   Paris   Montreal   Toronto
Delhi   Mexico City   São Paulo   Sydney   Hong Kong   Seoul   Singapore   Taipei   Tokyo

Editorial Director: Craig Campanella
Editor in Chief: Dickson Musslewhite
Executive Editor: Ashley Dodge
Editorial Product Manager: Carly Czech
Director of Marketing: Brandy Dawson
Executive Marketing Manager: Jeanette Koskinas
Senior Marketing Manager: Wendy Albert
Marketing Assistant: Jessica Warren
Media Project Manager: Felicia Halpert
Production Editor: Harriet Tellem
Production Project Manager: Clara Bartunek
Cover Designer: Suzanne Behnke
Cover Art: Shutterstock
Editorial Production and Composition Service: PreMediaGlobal

Library of Congress Cataloging-in-Publication Data
Danowski, William A.
  In the field : a guide for the social work practicum / William A. Danowski. — 2nd ed.
     p. cm.
  Rev. ed. of: In the field : a real-life survival guide for the social work intern. 2005.
  Includes bibliographical references.
  ISBN-13: 978-0-205-02227-4
  ISBN-10: 0-205-02227-8
 1. Social work education.   2. Internship programs.   I. Title.
  HV11.D357 2012
  361.3071'55—dc22

                                                                              2011018151

10 9 8 7 6 5 4 3 2 1   15 14 13 12 11

ISBN-10: 0-205-02227-8
ISBN-13: 978-0-205-02227-4

To past, present, and future social work students,
may you serve joyfully and well.

CONTENTS

PREFACE

TERMINOLOGY USED IN THIS BOOK: CLIENTS, PATIENTS, CONSUMERS

For years, professionals in the helping professions have debated about what to call the individuals they help. In hospitals, the word *patient* is generally used, and in some mental health settings, that label is often preferred. The terminology changes from setting to setting and varies according to geographic location as well.

In recent years, some have insisted that the word *patient* is demeaning and disempowering. Using the term *client* instead of *patient* is an attempt to help individuals feel less like victims of the system and to remind professionals that a *patient* designation does not suggest that individuals are entitled to lesser treatment or poor quality service because of a label they are given. Currently, more and more helping professionals use the term *client*, and sometimes the term *consumer* is used. The word *consumer* is derived from the idea that professionals need to help individuals recognize they are consumers of services and that they have rights, just as they do in buying any other service.

In social work practice, the term *client* is generally standard. The *Code of Ethics* of the National Association of Social Workers (NASW) states, "Social workers promote social justice and social change with and on behalf of clients." *Client* is used inclusively to refer to individuals, families, groups, organizations, and communities. Accordingly, the word *client* will be used throughout this book.

HOW TO GET THE MOST FROM THIS BOOK

In social work, we use the phrase, "begin where the client is," and accordingly, you can use this book to begin wherever *you* need to begin. Each person comes with different levels of skills, knowledge, confidence, and comfort, so feel free to use this book in any way that is most helpful to you.

You may want to skim the table of contents or index to find topics you need to read immediately. You'll probably skip around as you read. Feel free to write notes to yourself in the margins, dog-ear the pages, use paper clips, highlighters, or rubber bands to mark important pages or passages. I am personally a big fan of the small Post-its in all colors. If a particular idea or technique doesn't work for you, don't assume you misunderstood it or failed to apply it properly. Remember that different methods work for different social workers, and that each client is different from every other client. What works with one client may not work with another client. What is important is to begin building and learning new skills and techniques, and then applying this new knowledge.

While applying this new knowledge you may not be able to do things perfectly the first time you try. You may flounder, make mistakes, and often feel foolish. Nonetheless, you will gain the most from your field placement if you are courageous enough to step forward into new territory instead of staying totally safe with material you already know.

As a student in the field, please keep in mind two ideas about terminology: (1) regardless of your personal feelings, be flexible and use the term preferred by your supervisor and your setting; (2) whatever terminology you use, give your clients the best quality service you are capable of, help them to obtain their rights, and treat them with the utmost care, dignity, and respect.

Remember you are learning, and learning sometimes requires you to fail or feel unsure of the path you are taking. The goal of the field placement and supervision is to help you learn what works for you and your clients.

THE "RIDE OF YOUR LIFE"

"Learning can be a bitter-sweet experience, and often challenges you to grow stronger from difficult and uncomfortable situations."

Becoming a social worker is a learning adventure that has no beginning or end. Consciously or unconsciously, you've been preparing for this practicum all your life, and you will continue to learn and grow throughout your career as a social worker. You may not believe this, but you already know much more than you think you know. This is said with the understanding that there have been students who thought they knew it all only to find that they make serious errors working with clients. As you get oriented in your new placement and begin to relax, your own inner wisdom and all the messages your parents, teachers, and mentors have taught you will begin to surface. You'll become more and more comfortable with yourself, and learn to (1) apply the new skills and techniques, (2) let your own inner wisdom manifest itself, and (3) blend together your commonsense and skills.

Fact of life: we all learn differently and at different paces. Don't compare your progress to that of the student next to you at the placement or to those of your friends in other settings. Your life experiences are different from their experiences, so the process will be different for you than for them.

Be wary of making comparisons. Look only at your own progress or you'll get distracted from what you're here to do, and from the material you're learning, and from the agency you're fitting into. Yes it is true, you may have spent your entire life comparing yourself to your siblings, your neighbors, and the classmates next to you in Spanish. If you'll remember, comparisons did not help then, and they will help even less now. Comparing will only make you more nervous and anxious and get in the way of learning and being able to see the full picture. If you find yourself in this dark place of comparisons, talk to people you trust for validation. Speak to your supervisor and your field director or coordinator responsible for you and your agency placement. Discuss these feelings and explore simple solutions with them to get yourself into a better emotional state.

ACKNOWLEDGMENTS

I would like to thank the many individuals who as students have made this book possible. In particular, we would like to thank the following for the sharing of their experiences, and their feedback on our ideas and drafts: Leroy Ennis, Nicole Madonna, Dana Scalora, and Mary Lynn Schiller.

I want to thank Margaret Bourke for inspiring e-mail as I began writing the second edition. She wrote, "I truly enjoyed your book. It was a great help when switching roles from the classroom student to a social work intern. It helped lessen fears about interning, and guided myself, and other students in making that transition. I used it many times at my internship, and also writing my papers."

Grateful thanks are due to Christopher Tavella who spent countless hours editing my drafts. Without his efforts this book would have remained an idea unwritten. He helped transform the ramblings of this social worker into a book. And to my wife who listened to me numerous times concerning the book and gave me support by doing many household chores without me, particularly in the flower gardens.

But most of all, we owe a deep debt of gratitude to our many clients who have opened their lives to us and to our students. They teach us about real life and how to live it.

Before You Embark on Your Journey

Depending on the type of placement you are doing for your field work practicum, you may be learning how to conduct interviews and doing assessments or you could be leading groups, providing client advocacy outreach services, or setting up programs. As you know, in the field of social work, you can be working at the macro level or the micro level, or both levels at the same time. Your experiences will encompass an array of settings and with different populations, from individuals, families, groups, and community organizations. The ideal agency placement should give you a broad experience at both the macro and micro levels. But reality tells us that many things may not be available on the days you are in the agency. They happen on Tuesday and you are there on Wednesday. What you learn in your practicum is very important as it will become the foundation for your future as a social worker. As a student who has a desire to help others, you bring to your field placement (1) your appetite for learning; (2) the "book knowledge" you received throughout your program; (3) your learned and innate people skills; (4) your common sense and natural wisdom; and (5) your fearlessness to take on social injustice.

In the Field: A Guide for the Social Work Practicum will help you build your skills and give you a set of practical tools to use as you advance in your career as a social worker. You will learn how everything you do in field placement, and classroom sessions, including even your thoughts as you go to and from your placement, are all rich with learning opportunities. *In the Field* will help you learn to use even the most difficult and negative situations to your benefit.

During the early stages of the preparation of this text, I asked former undergraduate and graduate social work students to rank a list of issues and concerns they may face in the field (Table I.1). These issues will be addressed in the pages that follow and will be utilized to develop a basic skill set that you can use in your practicum and beyond.

THE COUNCIL ON SOCIAL WORK EDUCATION

You may have heard of this organization or been introduced to its role in the development of the field of social work. In the recent past, the Council on Social Work Education (CSWE) has had significant influence over social work education resulting in changes that impact what you learn in the classroom and the selection of field placements by your college or university. These changes have raised the bar for what is expected from your program, from your placement, and *from you*. You will see these changes reflected in your

TABLE I.1   Concerns of Field Practicum Students

1. Trusting yourself and your instincts
2. Learning how to learn from your environment
3. Preparing for new and unknown situations
4. Setting the stage for positive relationships
5. Dealing with fears and anxiety
6. Understanding and dealing with agency politics
7. Dealing with loss of idealistic ideas
8. "Finding your voice" with clients
9. Meeting paperwork requirements
10. Handling difficult clients and coworkers
11. Getting the most from your mentors
12. Channeling your anger in positive ways
13. Staying calm in the face of others' anger
14. Turning negative situations into positives
15. Understanding transference and counter-transference
16. Strengthening your boundaries
17. Making your age and experience (or lack thereof) work for you
18. Exiting gracefully
19. Evaluating what you've learned
20. Learning to think critically about your work with clients
21. Understanding that learning does not end with field work

program's Field Work Manual and in the standards for your practicum evaluation at midterm and term's end. You can locate a copy of the standards in the front of the book. They are the core competencies in the generalist practice model. Including these core competencies is not to overwhelm you but to help you understand the driving force behind your social work practicum experience. Additionally, these competencies will be highlighted throughout the text.

DO YOUR HOMEWORK

You will feel more comfortable if you research your new placement before you begin. Remember that having a working knowledge of your placement agency shows you are interested, motivated, and eager to start off on the best foot. If you were going on a job interview at a local company, it would be helpful to know the products it produces, how it markets those products, and its source(s) of funding. Professional helping agencies are very similar.

Social service agencies produce a product less tangible than a box or a crate, but what they produce is still a product. A child abuse agency's product would be protecting children; a mental health agency's product would be helping clients cope with their problems; or an agency working with the community could have a product that entails setting up after-school programs. These agencies market their services and have funding sources to which they are accountable. Often, a combination of these factors will dictate what kind of services an agency will provide and the kind of placements it offers. The more you know about your placement agency, the more you will know if it is right for you.

Being prepared may also lower your discomfort, or nervousness, to some extent. You will sweat less in the first few days and more importantly, it will be easier to ask questions and learn because you will not be paralyzed by your own anxiety.

You can get detailed information about the agency from your school or directly from the agency itself. You'll want to ask for some basic information about the agency and the physical building or buildings: Who owns the building? Who pays the rent? What is the funding source? How do individuals get access to the services? Are there criteria of eligibility to get services? Often, you will find community directories containing helpful information about local agencies. These and other source materials can be found in community and college libraries. Ask your college librarians for assistance, and they will direct you to the materials in the college library or tell you how to access the information on the Internet. It is commonplace to find agency websites that help you with information about the agency.

Remember the World Wide Web is but only one tool to use in gathering information. It is not the only tool. Nothing will replace talking to individuals with first-hand knowledge.

Of course, the more people you can talk with who are familiar with the agency, the more insight you may gain about how you will fit in your new placement. Whatever the sources you use, it is important to make a list of questions about the placement, the agency, and your potential supervisors.

Depending on your college and the agency, you may have the opportunity to see the placement setting and have an interview. I stress the term *interview*, because you are being interviewed by the agency's staff and this is similar to a job interview. They are looking to see if you are interested and whether your life experience and personality will be a fit with the agency, but at times this advance meeting is not always possible. Whether you ask your questions, either before or after your first day at the placement, is less important than knowing basic information about the agency. If you have the opportunity to meet with your supervisor and see the agency, read over your question list and see if you received an answer to each one. Write your answer next to each question. If there are questions you forgot to ask, couldn't remember the answer to, or the answers you received trigger new questions you want to ask, write them down. One useful tip is to use 3 × 5 index cards that are easy to put in your pocket. Jot down key words to trigger your memory of each question.

Remember you will be under stress and perhaps a bit anxious: new situation, new supervisor, staff names to remember—the perfect situation to forget things. Write your questions down.

Placement Interview Questions

Agency-related questions:

- Is there any material I can read about the clientele?
- What time would you like me to start the day?
- Am I required to attend any orientation program or trainings?
- Will I need a physical?
- What about a copy of any immunization or test such as PPD (tuberculin skin test)?
- Will I be fingerprinted and is there a cost?

- Do these need to be completed before I can start my placement?
- What is the agency's policy on cell phones? (They may not be allowed.)
- What is the dress code and are the clothes I am wearing appropriate?
- Do I need to sign in and out?

Student-related questions:

- Will I have a work space?
- Is there a break room?
- Where can I put my bag, books, and snack or lunch?
- Is there a staff directory?
- If I have to call in and you (the supervisor) are not here, whom should I speak to?
- If my supervisor (you may not be interviewed by the person who will be your direct supervisor) is off, am I permitted to be at my placement?
- If you (the supervisor) are not here and a pressing issue or problem comes up that I can't handle, what should I do? Whom should I consult?
- Are there any safety concerns I need to be aware of at this agency?
- Will I need any special materials?
- Are breaks and lunch at a set time?
- Where is the bathroom and do I need a key?
- If I am out for any reason, can I make up the time?
- Where do I park my car? Is there a parking fee? Do I need a parking pass?
- I will be using public transportation; can you tell me where the nearest train/bus stop is located?
- May I adjust my schedule to match the train/bus schedule?
- Will there be other students here at the same time or on the same day?
- If I think of any other questions may I call you?

Remember this is a two-way conversation. Whether it is during an interview or your first appointment with your supervisor, the supervisor or the representative of that agency will be asking you questions as well. You may want to prepare a brief resume that highlights key experiences. This can be an excellent jumping-off point for a discussion of your past experiences and how they will help you in this placement. If you have an opportunity to speak to students who have been at this agency in the past, find out if they were interviewed and what questions they were asked. Some typical questions might include the following:

- Can you come in on a weekend when there are special events?
- Can you be here in the evenings?
- Can you be here on days other than those the college has indicated as your placement days?

Often, these questions are related to special events such as a fundraiser, conferences the agency may be hosting, a presentation, or meetings the agency feels can be of interest to you and hence serve as good learning opportunities for you.

THE ELEPHANT IN THE ROOM

A sensitive area that often is like the elephant in the room that no one is talking about is physical disabilities. If you have a disability—a limp, you are legally blind, you have difficulty climbing stairs, or you have Muscular Dystrophy—whatever it is, don't wait for the agency supervisor to bring it up for discussion. Remember that some disabilities are easily seen, others can be hidden. Your supervisor as well as you will want to know how your disability might impact the staff, clients, and agency. For example, if you are hard of hearing, but manage well enough in one-on-one interactions by virtue of your lip-reading skills, no one may notice until you are in a group situation and are unable to follow all that is being said. This is not a minor point, especially if the agency you are working in does not have familiarity with clients with disabilities. If you are unsure about your particular disability, be open about it and discuss it with your director or coordinator of field placement at your college or university. He or she may have experience in this area and can provide meaningful input. Every college and university has a policy related to students with disabilities. Within that policy are guidelines that your institution and facility must follow concerning how to address the needs of the student. Colleges and universities also have staff assigned to validate the needs of each student identified with special needs.

If you have a disability that is validated by your college or university, you would already be aware of this information and you should be well informed as to your rights.

This college/university policy and the guidelines are important to you and the institution you attend to help you navigate its system and address your needs. But now you are literally in the field and whether your disability is recognized by the college or university or not you will need to address it with your placement agency. Persons with disabilities often forget because they live with them twenty-four hours a day and three hundred sixty five days a year.

PREPARING YOUR ATTITUDES

One of the most important things you can do to prepare for field work is to review your basic philosophy and attitudes. Showing up with a cooperative and helpful attitude will go a long way toward dealing with any fears or anxieties you may have.

"Every situation is a learning opportunity. Say yes to what life has to teach you."

Work at remaining nonjudgmental, even in your own thoughts. Stay in a mentally neutral, *observer* position. If you are constantly running "software" through your mind that says, "This guy's a jerk" or "That woman is crazy," your attitude will almost certainly leak out at some level and be perceived by the people around you. This may change the way others act toward you, without you understanding why. Remind yourself, also, that supervisors and others often have personal stresses and pressures that may cause them to behave in less-than-perfect ways. They may have health concerns, family problems, problems with employees, hassles and frustrations within the system, and attitudes that reflect poorly in their behavior, as well. This is why a nonjudgmental attitude is so vital. It will help you steer clear of others seeing you in a negative light and also allow you to have an opportunity to understand others who may appear, at first glance, to be negative or prejudiced. It costs you nothing to put the best face on a situation and refrain from judging. An old saying to keep in mind: "Seek truth, pardon error." Think also that given the same circumstances, you might act in exactly the same way. Your attitude will serve as the foundation for your actions and behaviors.

"The art of wisdom is in knowing what to ignore."

Through the years, I have supervised many different types of students. There have been motivated students, the kind who have positive attitudes and are willing to take on any kind of client or task. This type of student may or may not be an "A" student. I recall one student who struggled with academics and carried a dictionary because she was such a poor speller. In her placement work, she was upbeat and positive and did not let her academic struggles affect her field work. Another student had outstanding grades but struggled with family issues. She also was very motivated and took on any task asked of her and was always positive. However, she often showed signs of great stress; her eyes were bloodshot and she often seemed tired. Then there are students who appear to be positive and motivated, but struggle to keep up with the field work, documentation, and so on. The point is that successful students come in all *shapes and sizes*. What is more important is that you know which type of student you are and how you will be perceived by others.

What type of student are you? How will you be perceived by the clients, staff, and your supervisor?

"Be teachable. Be humble."

Know your limitations and be able to talk about them. It is always better to enter a field placement (as well as a new job) with an attitude that suggests that you don't know

"Learn to be a social worker first."

everything there is to know and that you are willing to learn. In general, supervisors are not nearly as concerned with what you know or don't know as with your ability to cooperate, your willingness to learn, and your willingness to work as part of a team. Most supervisors would rather have a willing student who is not well trained than a super competent one who will not listen, learn, or cooperate. Better to say, "I don't know what to do in this situation. Can you help me?" than to pretend to be more competent than you are or to barge in without knowing what you're doing and then not asking for help.

You Will Make Mistakes

"They're not doing it to you, they're just doing it."

Remember, you will make mistakes and they are an important part of the learning process. Don't try to cover them up. Ask for help, and learn how to do it right next time. Don't take things personally. It's not about you. Often when someone is angry with you or behaves badly because of something you said or did, that person is angry with someone else and you just happened to be there. Your actions cannot cause others to feel a particular way or do a certain thing—that's their responsibility.

Disagreements with Your Supervisor

When you feel that you disagree with your supervisor or a coworker, it is often wise to postpone your negative reactions. Instead, say something like, "What you've said sounds very important, so I'd like to think about it first before I act on it." This lets your supervisor know that you are carefully considering the message. It also allows you time to fully consider the message and to evaluate whether your initial disagreement was sound. If, after some contemplation, you still disagree, your supervisor will know that your disagreement wasn't based on purely emotional or impulsive grounds. In the meantime, you may gain a deeper understanding of the issue, and be able to formulate your response in a non-angry, nonthreatening, cooperative way. You may also be able to work out a compromise based on discussion and deeper understanding from you both. Always listen deeply, be fully present, and work at understanding what is said to you before you disagree or object.

Stay Out of Controversies That Don't Concern You

As a student, you're in a unique position to observe without the level of involvement of a staff member. Although agency politics may be uncomfortable, it's important to learn to let problems have their proper place without affecting you. Let other people's unpleasantness roll off you while you take care of your own business.

An important lesson to learn is how to use every opportunity as a learning tool. You can learn just as much or more from a negative encounter with someone as from a pleasant one. Remember the incident and learn from it. It is likely that, some day in the future, you will become a supervisor; you should make these events become part of your training and preparation for a higher level of authority in the future.

Through your words, actions, tone of voice, attitudes, and body posture, convey to your supervisor and coworkers that:

- you're here to learn, not complain.
- you're here to listen, not talk.
- you're a team player, not a diva.
- you're here to meet the clients' needs, not your own.
- you'll respect the supervisor, even if you disagree.
- you're willing to do what it takes to get the job done.
- You're dependable.

ASSESSING YOURSELF

Use a diary or a journal to assess your own strengths and weaknesses as you would assess your clients. Look at the techniques or defenses you use in conjunction with your weaknesses. Do these techniques enhance your learning, or are they geared to protect you and help you avoid confronting uncomfortable disconcerting knowledge about yourself? How might you respond to negative feedback from your supervisor during a supervising meeting? You may want to practice responding in your journal before you talk with your supervisor. In so doing, you will probably have calmed down, allowing for a more objective response. Ask yourself whether there is at least some truth in the information you were given. The key is to create an ability to hear what is being stated, and then work with that information—and not question it—in order to grow as a social worker.

Chapter 1 will cover in detail the issue of your safety while you are in your placement; however, keep in mind, while we discuss having an open, cooperative attitude, that it's your attitude that can affect your personal safety. Please don't think that because you are a social worker and championing social justice, you are safe from harm, or that people or clients will perceive you as interested in their best interests. Most times, a positive, cooperative attitude will help others see you as safe and not threatening.

BUILDING YOUR PROFESSIONAL WARDROBE

In planning what to wear, it would be helpful to know what level of formality your agency expects. What kind of clothing does your supervisor wear? How are your coworkers dressed? It is important to blend in rather than call attention to your clothing that is extreme in one direction or another. If you have little knowledge of a particular placement, ask your teacher or fellow students who have been in that placement.

"STRAPPED FOR CASH?"

It's a little-known secret that you can build a very professional-looking wardrobe by shopping at thrift stores: you can get everything you need for an amazingly low price. If you're not sure how to do this, ask a fashion-conscious friend to go shopping with you. Your friend will appreciate the challenge and can advise you about what looks good on you. My friend says, "The best thrift shops are in wealthy neighborhoods."

In general, think about what you would wear for a job interview and plan your professional wardrobe accordingly. Do not feel that you need to rush out and spend a lot of money to buy a whole new set of clothes. The contents of your closet can probably be updated with very little or no money. Take inventory of the suitable clothing you already own and make a list of anything you need to add.

One important issue with regard to clothing has to do with complying with safety regulations at your agency. By now, you should be familiar with the guidelines, or if you're not, ask your supervisor for a copy. For example, some agencies discourage or forbid high heels, dangling earrings, neckties, necklaces, or scarves. These items may pose safety concerns for your agency. Some hospitals have dress-code policies to protect the employees. An example is open-toe shoes being required to be worn with stockings, as an infection-control measure.

When I did a site visit for one of my students, I was surprised to find her in sneakers, blue jeans, and a hooded sweatshirt. I could not tell her from the adolescent girls at the shelter. Was this a professional social worker look? We could guess that the student felt it was important to have the teens accept her and the way she dressed went a long way to make that happen. However, it leads one to question, what other things has she done to earn that acceptance? Maybe nothing, but she has opened herself to these kinds of questions.

In any case, dress with good taste and in a way that is comfortable for you. In the first few days of your placement, it may be better to err on the side of formality than informality. You can always relax your standards once you are settled, but it would be embarrassing to be taken aside and told your torn cut-offs are a no-no.

> *A male student and I did not have the opportunity to meet before the placement began, which may have contributed to the problem. When we met the first day of the placement, the student was dressed in a wrinkled cotton shirt and blue jeans. The professional staff, at this setting, were all dressed in casual, yet dressy clothes—sport coats and ties for the men and dresses or dress slacks, tops, and jackets for the women. Not only did the student not dress professionally for this placement, it was clear that even after a few days, he had not noticed that his clothing did not fit in with the staff's. I called him into the office to discuss his clothing. After a short conversation, it was clear this student did own the appropriate attire but lacked awareness of the dress issue. This was not a good way to begin his placement with a new supervisor.*

In particular, female students need to dress modestly. That means no plunging necklines, short or slit skirts, exposed midriffs, or tight clothing. You may be working with clients with poor impulse control or who may think your fashionable clothes are seductive. They may even think you are sending sexual signals to them when you are just dressing in fashion.

> *On the first day of placement, a female student wore a tight, cleavage-revealing blouse. A male client came over to her and stared at her chest while engaged in conversation with her. Shortly after the incident, she came to my office in tears. Yes, the male client should not have done what he did; however, she, as a student, did not dress appropriately or professionally.*

There are times and situations where you can dress down, but still maintain good professional boundaries. This is essential whether you are working with clients at the agency, at a picnic, or on a therapeutic outing.

Ask for guidance about dress for special occasions. For example, there is a summer program for emotionally challenged adolescents who go to a local pool several times a week. The supervising staff were not permitted to wear bathing suits or use the pool. Clearly this program is concerned about professional boundaries and uses its dress code to reinforce them.

In addition to dress, check your mannerisms and use of humor. Students who act with their clients as they might with friends often confuse their clients. Clients may mistake your humor and friendliness for flirtation. Through your dress and manner, convey maturity, seriousness, and professionalism. Be careful not to send mixed signals. Clients may confuse your friendliness with sexual availability.

Technically Not Clothing

We cannot go on until we discuss body piercing and tattoos. They are part of many individuals' culture and may not be part of your clothing but they are part of your appearance. I am obviously not talking about the ones that are in private areas that are not normally visible. I am talking about eye brows, lips, nose, ears, arms and legs, and so on. You get the picture. What is the policy of your placement agency about body jewelry? Can your piercing cause you any risks while at this placement? Do you have any tattoos that others could perceive as offensive? Where are they located? Think this through. If they are on your arms and you are wearing long sleeves at the beginning of the placement, what will you do when the weather gets warmer? Will you switch to short-sleeve shirts? If they are on your neck and you wear your hair down, will you ever be wearing your hair up? Will the tattoos show?

THE *NOT-SO-AVERAGE* SOCIAL WORK STUDENT

As you travel through life you gather your personal history. It is as if you store it in a backpack you carry. In addition to life history, including learning experiences, good and bad, the backpack includes responsibilities you have collected, which may include a spouse, children, aging parents, debts, and one or more jobs.

> *One of my students had to feed two children breakfast, send one off to elementary school, the other to middle school and then check to see if her adolescent son came home and if he was asleep in his bed. All this before she set foot in the agency, I think her plate was full before she got to me.*

Older, mature students can appear more poised, more confident, and generally better equipped than their younger counterparts. Life experience can be misleading, creating a belief that the mature student is more prepared. Remember that both older and younger students have taken the same classes and have the same lack of experience in social work. However, being more experienced in life situations, older students will often not show their inner anxiety and uncertainty on the outside. The fact that you can hide your nervousness does not necessarily mean you are better prepared than students who cannot. Furthermore, your calmness may be a disadvantage in that your supervisor might think you are more skilled than you really are.

> *I was supervising an older student. She struggled through the first semester, eventually reaching the evaluation process. As she and I went over each area of her evaluation, she became increasingly agitated. When I addressed this behavior, she explained that she did not agree with my ratings. The student was unable to hear the message of her evaluation clearly. I reviewed the process and explained that she was expected neither to be an expert at this point in her training, nor to have learned all the tasks well at mid-year. She left the room very upset and eager to seek out her fellow students for emotional support.*

Students need to learn to be their own advocates, but confronting a supervisor without understanding the whole picture can be self-destructive. So, when did she cross the line? With each rating, examples were given that came from her process recording and supervisory conversations in which she discussed her work with her clients. Was the supervisor unfair? Had she been mislead prior to her evaluation? I will leave these questions unanswered for now. In this student's case, the student responded aggressively and repeatedly argued her viewpoint.

All students bring baggage that can both help and hinder them in their placements. The trick is to know when your life experiences are an asset and when they are a liability. Even your cultural background can be a liability. I will go into this more when I discuss culture and competence. You must also know how and when to apply your skills. Many supervisors would rather have a teachable, humble student of any age than an opinionated one who believes that he or she already knows what needs to be known. It is often easier to teach an unskilled person, than to work with someone who must be untaught ideas or practices that do not fit the setting.

You may feel more comfortable with the agency staff if you are close to their ages, and they may even speak to you in a different manner than they would to someone much younger. It is an easy trap to fall into for staff to treat you as a peer and forget you are inexperienced in social work. Don't misinterpret this familiarity to mean you are part of the staff. Be clear in your role as a student. Make it clear that despite your age, you are there to learn. If you are older than your supervisor, you might want to make it very clear that you acknowledge the supervisor's position and experience. Emphasize that you are able and willing to learn from someone younger than you. Your supervisor may be relieved that you won't automatically be a source of difficulty just because of the age difference. I will discuss the influence of age when I address gender and culture later in the book. For now, it is best that I leave you with this message: Don't assume.

Older students may see themselves as different and more experienced in life than their younger counterparts. But is this always true? Do they have greater knowledge than their younger students? It is obvious that older students have more life experience and they may have knowledge in some areas that younger students do not have. So yes, you are older, but be humble and cherish the experiences you have had, but do not assume you will have an easier time in field placement. In fact, it is quite possible that you may have a more difficult time. A more mature student may have more rigidly kept beliefs and attitudes, which will actually make the experience more challenging. All social work students share common concerns and issues, but there are variations in how those issues play out in field work placements.

HOUSE RULES

Much has changed in the past few years. We have experienced tragic events few others in history have. Times have changed; our world is very different now we did not have terms such as *9-11, Columbine, the Amish School shooting,* numerous college campus shootings and employee shootings. Each word or phrase conjures up thoughts and feelings of danger and emotionally charged events. We read about the male school teacher who sexually molested the 8-year-old school girl or the female teacher who is pregnant with a student's child. These are not easy times and many agency rules reflect today's world. House rules may seem silly or boring but they are there to protect you, the staff, and the clients who receive services at that agency. There may be security guards posted, video surveillance, or rules about touching clients. There may be an orientation requirement that involves listening to speakers and watching DVD on an array of topics from employee safety to infection control issues.

Orientation

If there is an orientation process, listen carefully. Are there any codes for medical emergencies or a code for "need help" when a client is at risk of hurting someone? What is the fire safety policy of your placement agency? What are you to do in an emergency? Do you call 911 or the safety department? Is there a list of emergency numbers, including fire, police, and ambulance? You may find that your placement has all, some, or none of these safety requirements. But even a good orientation may not prepare you for some events. While at her placement, one student was having difficulty with the computer printer and she was told to use the one in the office. Still struggling to get the printer to function, she pushed a button on the desk assuming it was a power on button. But she had activated the security alert and was soon surrounded by security personnel. I'll bet she never used that printer again. The point I am trying to make here is that orientations do an excellent job preparing you for your work in a placement but there can still be a few surprises.

Accountability

You will most likely be required to wear an ID badge, which helps the clients know who staff members are. Some agencies require staff to sign in. This is a way to account for who is in the building and could prove vital in an emergency such as a fire or hazardous spill. Sounds ridiculous? Several students of mine were in a building that had an unidentified chemical spill. The building was evacuated and everyone needed to be accounted for. Everyone was held and went through a cleaning process to be sure no one would leave the premises with contaminates on their clothing.

Some agencies are very formal in the manner clients and staff are addressed; others are less formal. You will need to be alert to the policy of your placement—formal or informal. This can be an important boundary issue with certain client populations. Ask your supervisor what is the expectation.

Personal Technology Usage

Cell phones and pagers are becoming so common that many agencies have developed specific policies addressing their use while on duty. Most agencies forbid their use while working with clients or in meetings. Cell phones that take photos are often forbidden in agencies that require client confidentiality. Before your cell phone rings while at your placement, ask about the policy. You can never go wrong by being proactive and turning your phone off when at your placement. Don't find yourself in the situation where you forget your phone is on and it rings while you are with your client or in supervision.

Transporting Clients

There are often rules regarding offering clients a ride in your personal car, even if the purpose of the trip is legitimate. Insurance liability, and personal safety, may require that you transport a client in an agency vehicle with another staff person to accompany you. Finally, what is the policy on home visits? I am introducing some of these issues now to heighten your awareness; we will pick this topic up again in Chapter 1.

What I have not mentioned here are the policies for record keeping and confidentiality. These topics are covered more extensively under the topics of paperwork and confidentiality, including the Health Insurance Portability and Accountability Act (HIPAA) in Chapter 2.

SUPERVISION, PLACEMENTS, AND SUPPORT FROM THE COLLEGE

There are certain realities that a student must often face. Over the years, we have all heard stories about difficulties with field work as well as stories about the wonderful moments. Situations range from students being assigned no clients or groups, limited supervisor time, or no supervisory time to students reporting quality supervision and support from other staff. There may be supervisors you wish you'd never known and others with whom you'll want to keep in touch with after your placement. So the amount of support you get during field work can vary a great deal.

Ideally, your field work will run parallel to your classroom assignments. However, today's colleges and universities provide an array of learning opportunities from weekend college to evenings and accelerated programs. Therefore, there are times when a student starts a placement out of sequence with class time. If you are one of these students, you can feel very isolated. You will need to make an effort to stay in touch with the college field work advisor. This can be through email or face-to-face interaction. The *how* is less important than the actual *doing it*. You must advocate for yourself and inform your supervisor of your needs over the course of the year. Supervisors and professors are mind readers. Students can struggle in field placement; yet, more often than not, do not talk to their supervisors or professors about their needs. Advocating for oneself is often more difficult than it would appear.

I began teaching the fall semester with several students who were in two different placements. Two students were in a counseling center, placed there in midsummer and were assigned groups that were actively running weekly. These students were being supervised and had plenty of material for class discussion and process recordings. Other students were placed in a shelter program where there was less structure and the on-site supervisor had been transferred. The students were not engaged in any client work and they had not brought this to the attention of the college field work faculty. Additionally these students were short of the required number of field work hours. This example illustrates the need to advocate for yourself.

> *A student was placed in an agency that had taken students over the years and therefore had a familiarity with our program, faculty, and student learning needs. Shortly after she began her placement, her supervisor had a family medical crisis. He was unavailable to the student and had not made any arrangements for coverage. The student did not advocate for herself and let several weeks pass. The college became aware when, in class, she casually mentioned she had not seen any clients or participated in any groups. The school intervened and advocated for her to the program director that appeared supportive. However, the director, overwhelmed in her role, was not able to help the student and again the student did not advocate for herself to the director or coordinator of field work. However, the director's knowledge of what had transpired led her to be proactive and the student was moved to a new agency. The student learned the importance of advocating for oneself and she learned an important social work skill.*

I hope this example demonstrates the importance for you, the social work student, to advocate for your needs in your practicum. If you struggle advocating for yourself, you may have just gained insight into how hard it is for some clients to advocate for themselves.

And, how will you advocate for your client?

We expect our clients to make their needs known. Doesn't that same rule also apply to social work students?

Field work placements are difficult enough without being in a strained relationship with your supervisor. What do you do if your supervisor tells you he or she is going on medical leave for six weeks? While this is not something for you to fix—it is the task of your supervisor to have a plan and discuss it with the college field faculty—it certainly may cause you to be concerned and perhaps angry. Talk about your feelings with your supervisor and especially with the person who will be covering for your supervisor during the six weeks.

Recently, I encountered two different experiences in the same semester. The first situation was with a group home supervisor who decided to leave the agency for personal reasons. A replacement supervisor had already been identified; the college had prior knowledge and the student was kept in the loop. In the second situation, the student did not fare as well. The supervisor was going on medical leave and did not tell the college or arrange for a backup. The student told the college that the supervisor would be out for an extended period of time and there was no plan for supervision. A supervision plan was put in place thanks to the student's sense of responsibility. Conversely, a less-assertive student may have been left on his or her own for six weeks—a recipe for disaster.

Again, you should always advocate for yourself with your supervisor and the agency. I have seen social workers who have taken on the responsibility for a student and then not been able to fulfill that responsibility. I have witnessed first hand social work supervisors unable to meet supervisory obligations due to medical reasons and family reasons. Similarly, I have also seen social workers leave due to changes in the organization, funding sources vanishing, and client referral sources depleting. As soon as you have knowledge of any of these or any other conditions that threaten your practicum experience, alert your college. It is likely you will know before your field coordinator or field director. You may be able to resolve the problem quickly with easy fixes (e.g., a simple transfer to another social worker to supervise you till your supervisor returns).

> *My student, Lee, was established in her practicum when her supervisor told her she would be out for surgery, but returning shortly after the holiday break. There was no other social worker in that department. After a discussion with the agency director, it was decided that the student would be assigned to a social worker in another department for supervision till her supervisor returned—easy fix. The student quickly developed a good working relationship with the new supervisor and continued in her placement. Unfortunately, the first supervisor's medical leave continued for an extended period of time and the backup supervisor accepted a position at another agency.*

Lee was fortunate that the backup supervisor was known to the college from a former agency that closed due to lack of funding. She agreed to take the student with her to the new agency. Sometimes the best-made plan fails and you must move a student. This is a very unpopular decision that social work program administrators try to avoid.

I want to mention one other scenario before we move on. It involves a supervisor who went out on medical leave the first day the student was at the agency. The supervisor was my coworker who was suddenly confronted with back surgery. She asked me to take her student until her return to work. I agreed. He was a great student who was eager to learn and quickly applied what he learned from our supervisor meetings. My coworker returned to work and he was moved to her supervision. He went reluctantly, feeling he had established a good rapport with me and did not want to start over. His reasoning was sound but there were two important factors that needed to be considered: first, I had my own student and as much as I enjoyed supervising him, it was a workload strain; second, and much more important, the returning social work supervisor had an intimate understanding of the program in which the student was assigned and she could offer him insights and learning I could not.

There are a lot of similarities between supervision and your working with the population at your agency. Later we will discuss in detail a concept called *mirror-mirror*. However, it needs to be briefly discussed here. Your relationship with your supervisor mirrors your relationship with your clients. If you are in a less-than-trusting relationship with your supervisor, can you be honest and share your experiences openly? The same is true for your clients. They need to trust you so they can feel safe enough to be honest with you about their needs.

Every placement has the potential for both positive and not-so-positive situations. Even the worst placement, however, can be rich in learning experiences. If you find yourself in a negative placement, talk to your coordinator of field work or the director of field work. He or she needs to know what you are going through, and may be able to give you helpful strategies to survive. Again, *you must learn to advocate for yourself.* You need to seek effective support as you can't learn if you are an emotional wreck.

With that in mind, what should you do if you are concerned that you can't handle the placement, or if you are frightened by or hate your supervisor? Advocate for yourself and let your supervisor or the field work faculty know what you are experiencing. The worst thing you can do is nothing. If you are anxious or frightened, speak to your supervisor—he or she is there to guide you. Remember, supervisors are not mind readers. Sometimes frequent short contacts or interventions with your supervisor can help you. Some supervisors are open to students showing eagerness to stop in and share their daily experiences. Others are more formal and prefer scheduled times to meet. In either case, be prepared with your questions and your concerns. The more open you can be about your personal experience as a social work intern, the better your supervisor can mentor and guide you.

There are a variety of ways to get supervision; the most well known is the formal supervisory model—a specific time when you meet with your supervisor to discuss process recordings and other issues. However, there are other paths to supervision that you may experience as well. For example, there are eager professionals in the agency often willing to lend a hand—perhaps the co-leader of your support group. Maybe you're overwhelmed by the agency's new record system but find that there are staff who are very good teachers of these tasks. Often you do not have to seek other supervisory assistance out, if you show a strong interest and are willing to learn, these additional supervisors will often offer their services.

LEARNING CONTRACTS

Learning contracts are a part of the supervisory experience and many colleges and universities require students to outline their learning goals while in practicum. Some students see this as a daunting task, others find it very easy. In either case, this is a skill that you will need to learn. Learning contracts reflect the work you will do with clients. What are their goals? How do you know they are achieved? How do you measure success if you have not established where you are now? Where do you want to be at the end of the process? I have been amazed over the years with the variety of learning contracts submitted to me for review. I have seen everything from copying the sample out of the social work field manual to very long and detailed plans. I want to impress on you that the learning contract is what you are planning to achieve as a student in the agency, so the process must be driven by you, not your supervisor. Of course, your supervisor can be a great resource in developing your contract.

Let's explore a variety of learning contracts, from the micro to the macro, to give you a foundation to build your own. Let's follow my wife's rule about dinner plans for guests—the KISS rule, which translates into "keep it simple stupid." Don't over think the process or you will end up copying the sample contract out of your field manual. Let's start with the design.

Select the landscape paper orientation on your computer and create a three-column table. (see Chart I.1.)

The following areas are the competencies the CSWE identifies as core competencies. These core areas will be reflected in your practicum learning experience and you will see them in your evaluation process. Use these as a guide for your learning contract. Of the ten core competencies you may experience more exposure and learning with some and less with others. A complete, detailed listing can be found at the beginning of

CHART I.1 Sample of Landscape Learning Contract		
Competence **(What am I to learn?)**	**Learning Strategy** **(How and where?)**	**Evidence of Accomplishment** **(How will I demonstrate it?)**
1.		
2.		
3.		

this book, but I've listed the ten competencies and some questions to consider below for your reference.

1. ***Professional Identity:*** Think about what will demonstrate that you look, act, and present yourself in a professional manner. Is being on time for meetings and appointments an example? Is there anything in the National Association of Social Workers *Code of Ethics* that addresses professionalism?
2. ***Ethical Practice:*** What demonstrates good ethical behavior at your agency? What does the NASW's *Code of Ethics* say? Are you respectful to the clients? How do you manage the issue of confidentiality?
3. ***Critical Thinking:*** This is not about coming up with answers but rather being able to see all sides of an issue and being able to evaluate how different solutions lead to different outcomes and consequences.
4. ***Diversity in Practice:*** Learn about the population you are working with at this agency. What are the characteristics of the population? How do culture and cultural practices affect what you do in working with clients?
5. ***Social Justice:*** This is not marching on Washington, D.C.; rather, it is about your clients as part of a larger picture. Do you have an understanding of how their place in society or in their family impacts their behavior? How will you learn about this issue?
6. ***Research-Based Practice:*** How will you show that you have an understanding of the importance of research as a tool to help you pick the best approach or treatments?
7. ***Human Behavior:*** How are you to learn about the individual behavior and the social environment of the population at this agency?
8. ***Policy Practice:*** How will you learn about the policies of this agency? What is the impact on the clients it serves?
9. ***Practice Contexts:*** What is your role at this agency?
10. ***Engage, Assess, Intervene, and Evaluate:*** On what levels will this be occurring and will it be with individuals and families? Will you be involved in groups and organizational activities, or even the community?

I caution you not to take my examples too concretely. They are merely questions to stimulate the thinking process. In the end, I doubt you will have ten items listed on your learning contract. At the time of your final evaluation, however, all of these core competencies will be addressed. Whether you have ten objectives, or five, be sure to include core competencies somewhere in your learning contract.

Always use the learning contract format that the college prefers or the one our placement agency supervisor prefers.

Your learning contract will (1) keep you focused on the goals of your placement, (2) tell you what you are to learn and how you are to learn it, (3) set the course and guide you—telling you when you are on track and when there is a need for a change of direction, and (4) help you and your supervisor focus on your practicum. Sit down with your supervisor to discuss the agency goals and the goals for their clients. Now you have at least one learning goal—to understand the complex goals of your clients. In filling in the contract, give details and provide strategies for how you will achieve these goals. Some of the strategies you can list will be your specific tasks such as your individual caseload of clients, assigned groups that you will run, home visits, family work, and so on.

I think most students see the development of the learning contract as an assignment—complete it, turn it in, and never look at it again. I understand this is what you have done with many assignments once you have completed them. You do it, and then move on to the next one. This document is different. It is meant to be a living document that needs to reviewed and updated as necessary. Agencies change over time and your learning needs will as well. You and your supervisor need to look at the learning contract frequently to determine if it meets your needs and progress or if it needs to be updated.

Remember, keep it simple and break your learning contract into components or small achievable pieces. The two samples (Charts I.2 and I.3) that follow are simply that—*samples*.

CHART I.2   Sample Micro Learning Contract

Competence (What am I to learn?)	Learning Strategy (How and where?)	Evidence of Accomplishment (How will I demonstrate it?)
• Client interviewing skills	• Meet with clients for intake process • Complete agency documentation	• Supervisory meetings • Process recordings
• Understand use of self in counseling	• Complete process recordings	• Feedback from supervisor
• Work as member of interdisciplinary team	• Participation in staff meetings • Shadow staff on home visits • Participate in outreach visits	• Process recordings • Supervisory meetings
• Assess client for strengths and areas of difficulty	• Process recordings • Development of treatment plan • Preparing agency documents	• Supervisory feedback • Able to present client in staff meeting • Provide case summary for school district

CHART I.3 Sample Macro Learning Contract		
Competence (What am I to learn?)	**Learning Strategy (How and where?)**	**Evidence of Accomplishment (How will I demonstrate it?)**
• Understand organization's structure and mission in community	• Interview staff • Read agency policy and procedure manual • Learn agency history • Review agency mission statement	• Supervision time • Able to participate in staff meetings
• Develop professional relationships with other agencies	• Establish meeting time and location • Prepare agenda items • Prepare minutes from last meeting	• Process recordings • Feedback in supervision
• Implementation of program	• Develop program proposal • Estimate budget • Establish time frames of development	• Supervisory meetings • Process recordings • Staff meetings
• Evaluation of progress	• Establish measurement tool • Collect data and analyze	• Report finding in staff meeting • Supervisor feedback

I've tried to provide you with a variety of possible learning experiences but by no means did I cover the topic in every detail nor would that be possible without knowing all of the types and varieties of agencies in which students do their practicum. My best advice, use your agency supervisor as a resource and support in the process.

NOTES

_____

_____

_____

_____

_____

_____

_____

_____

_____

_____

_____

_____

_____

_____

_____

_____

_____

_____

_____

_____

_____

_____

_____

_____

_____

_____

_____

_____

_____

_____

_____

_____

NOTES

_____
_____
_____
_____
_____
_____
_____
_____
_____
_____
_____
_____
_____
_____
_____
_____
_____
_____
_____
_____
_____
_____
_____
_____
_____
_____
_____
_____
_____
_____
_____
_____
_____

CHAPTER **1**

Making the Leap from Theory to Real Life

YOUR "MENTAL HEALTH FIRST-AID KIT"

- Structure your time, use a day planner; don't procrastinate.
- Do process recordings as soon as possible after a client meeting, group, or meeting.
- Build in time-off to do something for yourself.
- Take time to share and vent your feeling to peers.
- When did you laugh last?
- Don't take your placement home with you (easy to say, hard to do).
- Build some physical exercise into your week (yoga, dancing, walking, health club activities).
- When did you eat last?
- What did you eat?
- Don't set yourself up to solve all the clients' issues; be realistic about the short time you are in a placement.
- Learn to be patient and able to hold on to uncomfortable feelings.
- Start a journal and write in it at the end of each day at your placement.
- Supervisors are not perfect; if you think they are, they can only disappoint you.
- Share your day with supportive peers.

Good luck on your journey; may it be filled with rich, wonderful learning experiences. Being a social worker is not an easy profession; agencies have budget concerns and staff shortages and always have more clients than they can handle. But how many professionals can say they have had the opportunity to reach out and touch the lives of others, helping change and growth in individual clients, families, and agency policies?

TIME MANAGEMENT

Before we tackle some more social work practicum issues, we need to focus on the issue of time management. I have seen a wide range of time managers, from the obsessed who block out every second of the day to the worst in time management. Be organized, use an appointment book, and keep it current. Carry around 3 × 5 index cards to jot notes to yourself or keep a steno pad for notes and questions for your supervisor. Be on time for appointments and meetings; even be early. This is not another class where you can be ten minutes late and bring in your breakfast because you did not plan enough time to eat before the day is to begin at your agency. It does not matter if some of the paid staff do that; you are a social work student. Part of your practicum is developing and demonstrating professional behavior. You need to act professional at all times; there is no downtime.

A student came to my class twenty minutes into an hour-and-fifteen-minute class. He had an assignment that was due that day. I asked him why he was so late; he informed me he had overslept. When I raised the issue of time management, he told me he was using time management. I guess I should have stopped here but I pressed on and asked him to explain. He told me that the class assignment was first on his list last night. Sounds great, right? Well, not being able to disengage, I asked him what time he went to bed. Proudly, he told me as soon as he had completed his assignments—3 AM.

The expression is that time waits for no man or women! Or in our case no social work student. Be a good time manager.

You need to write your process recording sooner rather than later. The longer you wait, the more information is lost and the less feedback you will get from your supervisor when you discuss your process recording. This may be a generational issue as scholars begin to discuss the future of handwriting. Students want to type their process recordings and therefore wait till they are home with their computers. So much is lost from the time of the event you are using for your process recording till you get home. I recently had a student who handwrote her process recording and typed it on her computer when she got home. This is a great way to capture most of the information and still have a neat, spell-checked document, but it is time consuming. But remember to never use the client's name or any identifying information that could reveal the identity of your client; also, you may want to discuss this with your supervisor.

SAFETY

One of your first concerns should be your personal safety, as well as the safety of those around you. Insofar as possible, do advance preparation and ask questions ahead of time. Be aware of your surroundings. You should know something about the neighborhood where you're assigned. Are there safety issues to be aware of, such as night-time activity, drug-dealing, violence? Ask where you should park, if you drive to the agency, and find out if you need an escort in or out of the building, particularly after dark. Many agencies are located in areas that may see a high rate of street crime and violence. Being a social worker does not protect you from crime in the area being directed at you. Too often, we hear news about random street violence.

Assess the climate of your placement. Remember that not every person who walks into your agency is necessarily an innocent person there for help. It is possible that some may be there to help themselves to your purse or wallet. If you carry a purse or bag, either keep it with you at all times or ask where it can be securely stored while you are on duty. The same rule applies to your cell phone or perhaps *PDA (personal digital assistant)*.

With many agencies, there may be a high risk factor for violence directed toward you from clients, or even family members of clients. You may feel your client would never hurt you because you have a good relationship but that does not mean the client's family members or friends have warm feelings toward you. In fact, they may perceive you as a scapegoat, that you have somehow directly or indirectly caused problems for their family member or friend.

Some clients are voluntary, meaning they come to the agency by their choice; others may be mandated by court orders, including treatment or jail mandates, to do so.

Still others may have services forced on them by agencies designed to protect the public, like child or adult protective agencies. Persons in these situations may not experience you as a positive presence in their lives.

Recently, a student wrote in her process recording about her client who was involved in the court system for past illegal drug use. That day the client was told she had failed to follow through on her court mandate, which meant she would be going to jail as soon as she went into the court room. She ran from the building and sped away in her car. No one was hurt, but what would have happened if the student had tried to stop her? The student was shaken by the event and her own surprise by not expecting what happened.

There is often a false sense of security in social workers who believe that because they do good in the world they are somehow magically protected from harm from others: how could anyone be angry or violent toward us when we are there to help? In fact, that feeling of being a do-gooder can cause you to be less vigilant, thereby increasing your chances of being a victim of violent actions. You need to recognize we are living in a society that has seen an increase of violence in general and in the workplace in particular.

I recall a group of clients with mental illness on their way to nearby vending machines. I was in the hallway heading that direction to interview another client. As the group of clients passed, a woman took a fisted swing at me, missing me only by an inch. I was lucky. I should have been more alert in assessing that this woman was agitated and that her behavior was likely to spin out of control.

We all want to be seen as *the good guy*, but the reality is that sometimes social work teams make decisions that are seen as negative or even catastrophic to their clients. Teams sometimes decide to hospitalize people, remove children from a home, and so on, so you may not always be seen as the helper you believe and know yourself to be.

Surprisingly, there may even be a possibility of violence between coworkers. It is likely that the staff you will work with represent many different ethnic groups, with different levels of education and job responsibilities, from clerks to PhDs and MDs. If there is a conflict, it is your responsibility not to try to stop an argument or a fight but to quietly disappear and bring help. You are not exempt from violence because you are *the student*.

Many agencies have strict dress code requirements related to safety. Specifically, you may find that high heels and slick-soled shoes are prohibited, along with anything worn around the neck that might make the wearer vulnerable to choking. Also, often discouraged are dangling earrings, attention-getting jewelry, or suggestive clothing, such as scoop neck tops, tight-fitting clothes, and clothing where your underwear show above or through the clothing.

A student recently asked me if her stylish earrings would be an issue at her placement. I answered the question in two ways: first, it is not important what I think but what her agency supervisor thinks about her issue; second, think about the agency population; is it a population that may want to reach out and grab a dangling object? What is important here is simply the fact that the student was thinking about her dress.

Avoid trouble by monitoring your environment and staying out of difficult situations. Prevention is an important policy to follow. If you sense trouble brewing, probably the best thing you can do is to quietly bring help. Do not attempt to intervene in arguments, fistfights, or in any situation that seems to be heating up.

Another way you can increase your personal safety is to help clients to feel safe with you. Do not aggressively confront, threaten, or otherwise back a client into a corner, either physically or verbally. Always allow clients to keep their self-esteem and self-respect intact. Allow them a way to interpret situations in non-threatening ways. Remember to buy time by temporarily smoothing situations over. You can get to the root of a problem later after consultation with your supervisor. Ask for any kind of help you need and don't be afraid to apologize or back down in a sticky situation.

At the first meeting with your supervisor, ask about:

- Staff experiences in the neighborhood
- Where to park
- Dress code (what and what not to wear for safety)
- Risks with your client population
- The agency's experience dealing with violence in the building
- The home visit policy and what have staff experiences have been
- Agency training to handle aggressive and violent situations
- Training available to you as a student

My student was at her placement co-facilitating a group for children around the age of twelve. Suddenly, one of the students without warning jumped to his feet and fled the room. A computer and a desk suffered ill fortune as the student fled down the hall.

This real-life event helps to illustrate some issues: Why was the child upset? What triggered the sudden change in behavior? Was he hurt physically by his actions? What impact did this have on the other children in the group? And what triggered the events? How well did the staff handle the situation? And what was it like emotionally for the staff involved? I can tell you the student could not wait to write this process recording.

Safety Rules

Some of this material was mentioned earlier in the Introduction under Home Rules, but your safety may depend on it, so let's review some of the rules and expand to other topics. I want to remind you about different emergency codes to alert staff to dangerous situations. I was in a meeting recently where it was mentioned that a seasoned employee did not know the emergency codes of the hospital. Do not find yourself in this situation! Ask if there are any code systems; often you will find a color system, such as *code blue* for a medical emergency. During your orientation to the agency, safety as a topic may be covered. Be sure to pay attention and ask questions when appropriate. *Safety* refers to many different areas, including fire as well as personal safety. Or you may find the agency uses a code phrase, like "Dr. Redstone, please come to the office. . . ." Other agencies may not have developed systems because of function or size; that does not excuse you from asking your supervisor what to do in an emergency.

Home Visits and Travel

Similarly, what is the agency's policy on home visits to clients and transporting clients in vehicles? Veteran social workers have found themselves in volatile situations, resulting in policy changes in their agencies. The home visit policy can vary from expecting you to go alone, or making traveling in pairs a must, to even having the police meet you at the home. The policy for transporting clients can also vary from using your own vehicle to using only agency vehicles and requiring that more than one agency staff person accompany the client. The wide range of policies reflects the diversity of agencies. You need to know the policy of your agency; if you have concerns about a situation, discuss it with your supervisor.

A student asked if she could discuss her recent home visit experience. She had been on many home visits by herself and was very comfortable with this model. She went on a routine home visit to one of her clients. When she got there, she found that the client had been drinking, and was hostile and verbally threatening to her. She left immediately, returned to the agency, and reported the matter to her supervisor.

This was an emotionally charged event; even after she had processed it with her supervisor, she still needed to process more. The lesson learned here is that circumstances can change: be prepared to act to protect your safety and the safety of your client. A home visit to a friendly elderly woman can change suddenly because a family member drops by to visit.

A student was asked to do a follow-up home visit. She had been to this home many times to visit the elderly woman who lived with her daughter and son-in-law. The agency had placed the elderly woman in a senior program at her home. It was suspected that the daughter was being abused by her husband and the student was asked to do a home visit when the daughter would be home alone to see if the daughter would address this issue with her.

Do you think the student should be placed in this situation? Or do you see this as a wonderful learning opportunity that does not come along every day?

When the student called the elderly woman's home to set up the home visit, her daughter's husband answered the phone and wanted to know the purpose of the visit.

Never go on a home visit or have face-to-face contact with family members without the knowledge of your supervisor at your agency.

What would you say to him? The home visit did occur and the husband took the day off work to be there. What next, if anything, do you think should be done?

You can find a wide variety of approaches to the issue of safety, from required trainings before you are allowed to start your agency practicum to much less. If your placement agency does not have a formal training program, it is your responsibility to speak to your supervisor about the subject; don't wait for your supervisor to bring it up.

Some Safety Tips:

- The best predictor of behavior is past behavior. Read your client's chart and discuss his or her behavioral issues with your supervisor.
- What is the agency's policy about you being alone in the building?
- Never block your client's exit route when you are meeting with him or her. Sit in a neutral place, where you both have access to the exit.
- If your client is upset before you begin your meeting, make other staff aware before you begin. You may want to leave the door open.
- If your agency uses any type of device that you carry with you, such as a personal alarm, make sure you have it with you and you are familiar with how it works.
- Never attempt to reach out and touch an angry, agitated client.

Cynthia Garthwait (2008, 57–58) discusses Irwin's four stages of crisis management in her book. If your agency practicum does not have training or some form of safety education, I suggest you start with this material and ask your supervisor for direction to other literature on the topic.

Health Precautions

You may be working with a client population often referred to as *at risk* or *high risk*. Whatever term is used in your agency, you must have a full understanding of what it means in relation to the clients you will serve. I want to highlight this point for your safety when working with clients in general. When we take a first-aid class, universal precautions are taught. If you take a CPR class, you will be taught universal precautions, because of the risk of being infected with acquired immune deficiency syndrome (AIDS). This topic may be adequately covered in your classroom but in the field we often do not think in terms of universal precautions. Discuss the various risk factors that apply to your placement with your supervisor and develop a good working knowledge of these risks. Remember, knowledge is power. Develop an understanding of how this disease and other diseases are transmitted; you do not want to be fearful in your placement because you have been asked to work with an individual with whom there may be some health concerns.

We as social workers often provide services to populations that have multi-dimensional problems. For example, a homeless individual may also have health problems, such as tuberculosis or hepatitis. Again, I emphasize, get a good understanding of the population in your placement agency; knowledge is power. As mentioned in the Introduction, you need to know if you are required to have immunizations along with a PPD test (tuberculin skin test) prior to your placement. There are more examples that I could provide but I believe I have made the point that you have to work comfortably with the clients in your placement and you need to feel safe. Being anxious in a new placement in one thing but safety concerns can paralyze your learning. In such cases, ignorance is not bliss.

Quite recently, I learned that pregnant women should avoid exposure to anyone who is receiving radiation treatments, such as clients suffering from prostate cancer. I am not an expert in this area so I offer a suggestion; any relevant health history should be part of your meeting with your supervisor. You need to protect yourself: the only person who can do that is you. Before you start your placement, see your doctor and discuss your health and any potential areas of concern. Be sure to discuss any concerns with your field placement director. Do not wait till you are in your placement and see if something comes up: this is a bad plan!

If your placement is in a community hospital that provides medical care or in a skilled nursing facility (SNF), be aware of current health care concerns about super bugs. These are not the only places you need to be concerned. The same concerns exist if you are doing your practicum in a psychiatric hospital, just to a different degree. MRSA, *Methicillin-resistant Staphylococcus aureus* and/or C-Diff, *Clostridium difficile* are major health concerns. There is a large volume of information on the web covering these infections, so I will not cover that topic; however, learn how to protect yourself. We know that proper hand washing is part of good prevention and you can learn the proper technique for hand washing at your agency orientation. If this is not available to you, go to the college health center and speak to a nurse. They have been trained in the proper technique of hand washing and can give you a demonstration. Also, the Internet is a great resource. Website sources, such as the World Health Organization, fondly known as WHO, www.who.int, are helpful. Your supervisor is also a source of information.

When you go to a patient's room and there is a "use protective gear" sign on the door, this means either you or the patient is at risk for some type of exposure. If you are unsure as to what to do, ask someone at the nursing station or return to your supervisor for further instructions. Use the same procedure before entering a negative-air-pressure room.

If in doubt ask, never assume!

MISTAKES: ERRORS OF TECHNIQUE VERSUS ERRORS OF THE HEART

Before their first field placement, many students worry if they possess enough knowledge. They often are certain that they do not know nearly enough about theories and techniques. Remember this old saying: "Our clients will forgive us for errors of technique, but they will never forgive us for errors of the heart." If your heart is in the right place, if you sincerely want to help your clients, and if you are humble enough to admit your mistakes and apologize, you will learn the techniques you need as you go along.

A client wanted me to help him make a phone call. Being very new in my placement, I was afraid that would be against the rules or somehow not appropriate. I told him "no" in no uncertain terms, because we had to concentrate on my agenda. He became angry with me, and seemed to withdraw and shut down. I didn't have a good feeling about the situation. When I talked to my supervisor, she suggested I apologize to him and help him make the call as soon as possible. He seemed very relieved when I told him how sorry I was that I did the wrong thing. We made the call, and ever after, he was much more open and cooperative. My apology seemed to make a huge difference in the quality of our therapeutic relationship. Even though it was hard to admit I was wrong, my supervisor helped me to correct a serious error.

What you have learned from your classes and textbooks is very important. That knowledge serves as the base of the pyramid upon which you will build your career. However, in the helping professions, it is impossible to learn everything you need to know from books and classes. You learn by doing. You learn by experience, by getting your feet wet, by observing, and by making mistakes. Life and your clients will continue to teach you what you need to know throughout your entire career. You will keep on learning and growing, no matter how many years of experience you attain. Just keep your mind and heart open, and the lessons will appear.

Treating your clients with respect and dignity is essential to being a good social worker. Your clients know when you are sincere and truly want what is best for them, without the exact words ever being spoken. Treating others with respect and dignity applies to macro practicum as well. If you are leading a meeting of several agencies, your role, behavior, and attitude can be critical.

Shortly, I will begin to share some actual process recordings with you to illustrate certain points with real-life experiences. Note that these recordings are not necessarily the ideal way to handle a situation, but an example of how a social worker actually reacted.

PAPERWORK

You will find at least four categories of paperwork activities occurring at the same time: first are the papers you need to produce for your college or university. Make your on-site supervisor aware of these in order to give him or her time to direct you if you need assistance. This may begin in the form of a learning contract, which many social work programs require. Your supervisor is a resource; use him or her for input. If you ask for help when your paperwork is due in just a few days, expect little or no help. You will also be sending the message that you are not responsible enough to plan ahead, keep track of your tasks, and complete them in an orderly fashion. Your supervisor may be very helpful if given time to think about what you need.

The second kind of paperwork is advocacy for your client, including Social Security forms, forms to replace lost green cards, unemployment papers, Department of Social Services forms, public assistance forms, or any other kind of paperwork they need help with. This type of paperwork strikes at the heart of what it means to be a social worker. Often referred to as *concrete services*, this kind of paperwork is crucial to your clients' well-being. As a social worker you may find yourself helping your client in this manner. We advocate for our clients. We help them do things they need help with. Ask your supervisor or other staff about the common types of advocacy paperwork at your agency.

The third type of paperwork is the documentation paperwork required by your agency. Documentation is a critical part of agency work and it is important to remember that each piece of paperwork becomes a legal document. It is important that you understand the documentation needs of your agency from day one. The kind of paperwork you will do depends on what kind of agency you have been placed with; for example, federal, state, private, not-for-profit, school-based, specialty programs, or grants, just to name a few, all have different requirements.

Increasingly becoming more popular is the electronic record keeping system. While visiting someone in the hospital you may have seen the nurse take the patient's vitals and then enter that information on a computer in the patient's room. Some electronic record keeping systems are partial, meaning the complete client record is not computerized. An example of this partial record could be tracking vitals. In other systems, the entire client record is computerized and referred to as *paperless documentation*.

Access to computerized client records is well guarded to protect the client from any breach in confidentiality; therefore, your access may be limited. On the other hand, if there is an expectation you will be completing these computerized forms, you will go through the process of being granted access. This can involve signing forms stating you will protect against others gaining access, finger printing for scanners, and changing passwords often. Often this process is followed in training sessions.

Many supervisors encourage their students to read client records to get an idea of the kinds of paperwork needed. If your supervisor does not offer to show you actual client records, you might ask to see examples of completed paperwork. As you will be required to do paperwork, looking at such examples will help you know exactly what is expected of you. Ask questions. For example, do the forms or paperwork have detailed categories to be filled in or are they free-form? Make notes on a blank form or make yourself an outline to follow. Show the outline to your supervisor and get his or her feedback on its completeness. Rewrites are time consuming and not a rewarding activity, even though you will often find yourself doing them. You will need to know what forms to use, and how often they are to be completed. Some agencies have standardized questions that are asked of all new clients. You may be expected to complete these forms as part of your practicum.

It is important to note recent changes in documentation issues. You will see that most documentation is date stamped either in a computerized system or by the staff person. You now see in many agencies an expectation that you not only date stamp your entry but also time stamp it. The driving forces behind this movement are not important, only that you are aware of your agency's expectations.

> Your client's chart is a legal document and needs to be treated in that manner. This means, treat the chart with care; be neat; make sure the content is accurate; and that it presents your client in his or her best light.

Writing in a Client's Chart or Record

Kagle and Kopels (2008) have a list of what they consider important principles for good record keeping. I want to share a few of them with you. Some or all may be useful to you as you begin to document information.

- Is the client involved?
- Have you considered the cultural context of the individual?
- Is there a good assessment and is it impartial?
- Who is the source of the information; does it tell me who the informant is?
- Is the written material well written?

If you demonstrate these five basic principles in your paperwork, you will be off to a solid start.

Generally speaking, each time you have contact with a client, whether it is a structured, face-to-face session, a telephone conversation, or even a significant interaction in the hallway, that contact needs to be documented. Some of this documentation may be related to agency billing. Your documentation in the chart leaves a trail of activity; this is valuable if someone needs to work with your client in your absence. That person will know about the last contact and the content of that contact. You will find value weeks or months later when you and your client reflect on progress, as you will have the documentation to trace the progress or lack thereof.

If not offered, ask to see client records to begin to understand the forms the agency uses, the intervals in which forms need to be completed, and the structure of notes. In some placements, you are asked to write notes in rough-draft form on scrap paper. Your notes are then reviewed by your supervisor, with input to help you rewrite the note. In some cases, a supervisor might rewrite the note or help you put it into final form. When you have demonstrated your ability to write acceptable notes, you may have less supervision concerning them.

Other supervisors may discuss the necessary content of a note and then let you write it on your own. Remember: you haven't written chart notes before. This will be your first time, so don't expect to write a perfect note. Soon you'll become comfortable with the process and be able to write notes that fulfill your agency's requirements.

Progress Notes and Documentation

The purpose of a progress note is to document the client's progress (or lack of progress) toward particular goals. Ask your supervisor about what you say and don't say in a chart note. As these are legal documents, you must always keep in mind that it is possible that some day, your note or notes may be read out loud in a courtroom, so write the note accordingly. Ask your supervisor how brief or expanded the notes should be. Given current changes in privacy laws, some agencies prefer that you document as briefly as possible in order to protect the rights of the client.

Another possibility is that at some point, clients may ask to read their own charts. In the past, it was standard procedure not to allow a client to read his or her records, but state and federal laws are changing on this issue. Would you be comfortable with your client reading what you have written about him or her?

Regardless of the format of the note, make sure that above all, the content of the note is accurate. Take care to document only what is necessary, and consult with your supervisor if you think the content of a note might harm the client either now or in the future. For the future protection of the client, you may be asked to write notes in a vague summarized fashion. There are ethical issues here that need to be discussed; I suggest you take the time to discuss them with your supervisor and this is wonderful material for classroom discussions. For example, you might not write in detail about a past event that might inadvertently prejudice a less understanding worker against the client.

There are many formats in which a note can be written; a SOAP note is one such example. You will find there are many more acronyms for notes that I have not mentioned but their goal is all the same: to present the client problem, show what has happened, and where to go from here. A SOAP note stands for subject, objective, action, and plan. The subject can be a parent getting custody of his or her child. The objective is to determine how he or she will achieve the goal. The action is what he or she has been doing, including the level of progress and the plan from this point. SOAP notes and other designs are discussed by Kagle and Kopels (2008). I suggest looking at their material as it can help you understand the different approaches to address the same issue. Kagle and Kopels also discuss target behaviors and measurability of progress—critical issues for today's agencies. Your agency may use a particular format that you will be expected to follow.

At the risk of repeating myself, it is important that I mention that your notes, or whatever type of documentation, be dated and indicate what time you had the conversation with the client. Recently, oversight organizations such as The Joint Commission and the Center for Medicare and Medicaid Services have been stressing the date and time stamp on documentation.

Sloppy Documentation

I have seen this done many times: things entered into a client's record that have not been validated, such as arson. You have a moral and ethical responsibility to report and record with as much accuracy as possible.

A social worker came to me and reported that there was an entry in his client's records that the client had set fire to his home. He was making a referral for housing for the individual and knew this would impact his client's chances of being accepted. This social worker took the time to interview the case manager and others only to find out there had been a fire in the home at an earlier date and it was not set by the client. This is important information; if not corrected, it would have impacted this client for the rest of his life. And every time he denied the event, how would he be perceived? as a liar? Documentation is important and I just want to heighten your understanding on this topic.

Group Notes and Meetings

Often, the leader of a group activity is expected to document the group's activity in the form of a note in the client's record. Electronic record keeping often will allow you to write one note that is then populated to the records of all members of the group. You can see this is a time-saver for the writer but it does not allow you to customize the note on any particular client. Also, be very careful not to mention anyone by name or use any indentifying information that would suggest an individual in the group. Check with your supervisor if you find yourself leading a group and documenting that event. You may need only a summary of the group event and it will not be placed in any client records. But be sure to follow the policies of your agency. Here are three basic elements in documenting a discussion: (1) the topic; (2) what was discussed; and (3) what was the outcome/action as well as who is responsible for any follow-up. The function of the last part is important in follow-up meetings to ensure the action was completed and the topic is closed.

Recording Errors

As for documentation, I want to bring your attention to a product that got a social work student into trouble. Do not use any kind of white-out on your forms or notes. Ask your supervisor for the proper procedure to correct a mistake in a client's chart or formal paperwork. You may not want to discuss a mistake or misspelling with your supervisor, but do not use white-out. Find out your agency's policy in making corrections. The general rule, draw a line through the word and write the correct one next to it. Your agency may also require you to initial the correction. Again, don't forget that the client's chart is a legal document, and you do not want to create a situation where someone can say that you were trying to hide something, no matter how trivial the detail or how innocent your motivations.

A supervisor explains: One of my students was not the best of writers or spellers and had made a spelling mistake in a client's progress note. I read the note she had written and co-signed her signature, as is the policy in my agency. A few days later, the client's doctor came to me concerning something written that day by my student that I had not yet seen to review, discuss, and co-sign. When I looked at the new note there was a word that had been whited out, but the situation grew worse when I noticed that the prior note I had

Tips concerning paperwork:

- Know which forms are required and which are not for every client.
- Know how often forms must be completed (every three months, six months, yearly, or every visit)
- Ask for a written reference guide at the agency for the structure of notes and forms. Make notes on the blank forms if you can, or take careful notes.
- Know what content is needed in a note, and what content should be omitted (and why).
- Know your agency's note format.
- Don't use white-out products.

co-signed had also had altered with white out after I co-signed it. Once I stopped hyper-ventilating, I called the student in to my office to explain herself.

The first mistake was that as a supervisor, I had apparently not made it clear to her that white-out was never to be used. The second error was that the student should never have altered a note that a supervisor had co-signed.

The incident became a learning experience for both the student and for me as a supervisor. The student was trying to present the best note possible, but ended up with more problems than she had bargained for.

There is an expression in the field: "if it isn't documented, it did not happen."

A final comment on client charts and documents that are part of the record: they are legal documents and are never to leave the agency without proper authorization. As a student, never remove documents from a client record for your use in a classroom assignment. I have seen a student lose his placement because he took home a client's record to prepare an assignment on cultural differences.

PROCESS RECORDINGS

An important category of paperwork is your process recordings, a time-honored tradition in social work. Your process recordings are invaluable tools of learning.

Your supervisor may give you a form he or she prefers or your college or university may have a format. Sometimes it is included in the program field manual. In the absence of a formatted process recording, there is a basic structure that can be made up on any computer. With most word processing programs you have the ability to make tables; create a simple five-column table that will fill a page in landscape format. If you get stuck, ask a friend to help.

The top categories can be arranged as your supervisor prefers. Remember to write your name, the date, and the number the pages at the top of the process recording even if you staple the pages together.

Generally, your process recording will begin with a cover sheet that guides the reader to the meeting content. That information sheet may vary but it will cover some basic information

- Client
- Location of interview
- Purpose of the contact
- Basic client description
- Pre-engagement discussion

This format below will work well for a single client, a family, or even a group setting.

He Said/ She Said	Feelings/ Reactions	Analysis of Feelings	Supporting Literature/ Evidenced by	Supervisor Comments

However, if you are doing your placement in a macro setting, I suggest a different format for your process recording of meetings you attended or participated in. The structure of the process recording is very different. The cover sheet will include the following: location, participants, purpose of meeting, and structure/format of the meeting. However, the content of the process recording form is very different.

The table below will give you some guidance on how to address process recordings other than the direct client meeting.

What Occurred	Student Reflections	Self-analysis	Interpretation of Meeting/ Evidence Based	Supervisor Comments

Within the first column the student must include introductions, if any, level of participation of members, decision making, and what was covered. The difference for the student is that the client is the group or an organization, not an individual. Even if you are not in a macro placement, I suggest you try doing a process recording on a meeting you attend, such as a student case conference, a treatment planning meeting for a client, or a discharge or placement meeting or a court hearing.

Remember, do it sooner not later for the best content of process recording.

You will fill in the appropriate columns, and the supervisor will add comments under "Supervisor Comments," either in writing or verbally in the supervision session.

Present yourself to your supervisor as an organized person. When you write your process recording, did you remember to number the pages and put your name and the date on the top of each page? Don't forget to make copies of your process recordings. If your supervisor gives you the process recording back with his or her comments before you meet, make a copy of those comments as well. That way when you meet, you will each have a copy of the same material during the supervision discussion and can easily refer to the same material together.

My supervisor always tells me, "When you come to supervision, bring two copies of the process recording." One of my peers did not do this. He would enter the room with one copy and the supervisor would ask him to go to the copier and make another copy. When he returned he would have two copies, but they were now out of order and disorganized. This is not how you want to present yourself to your supervisor.

Best Practice

One of the columns on your process recording will be *evidence-based or best practice*. This is where you put the supporting literature for what is happening in your meeting. Your director of field work or the coordinator will guide you and this will be discussed in class. It is important to know that what you are doing is based on some evidence. It is no longer acceptable to do something just because you always did it this way.

A representative from a day program for individuals with chronic schizophrenia told me that the clients needed to attend five days a week to remain stable and not get re-hospitalized. The agency running the program lost their lease and were temporally housed with another agency. The clients could be shuttled there only once a week. Ironically, the program's hospitalization rate did not go up.

This is a good example of not knowing what is in the literature and making assumptions. Agencies are now paying closer attention to this issue because of requests for reimbursement from third parties.

NOTES

NOTES

CHAPTER 2

Ethics

It is important as a student to be familiar with social work code of ethics. When I search for *code of ethics* on Google, I get 23,300,000 hits. And if I refine my search to *code of ethics for social workers*, I get 2,000,000 hits. I am not sure what type of statement that makes, but it is a statement. Every organization has a code of ethics from psychology to teachers. I will address three organizations in this chapter: the National Association of Social Workers (NASW), the American Board of Examiners in Clinical Social Work, and the Society for Clinical Social Workers. I will not bore you with how there are three different social work organizations and the politics; it is sufficient that you are aware that there is more than one organization, and, depending on where your career takes you, you may be a member of one or more of these organizations. The focus here is social work code of ethics. And our discussion will begin with some basic concepts you will later see are embedded in the code of ethics. In the "Ethics Code" section of the American Board of Examiners in Clinical Social Work's website (www.abecsw.org), we find an important sentence: "Ethics are precepts that guide the moral conduct of professionals; they are not the same as practice standards. . . ."

Later in this chapter, I will focus on the laws that govern sharing of information, better known as the Health Information Portability and Accountability Act (HIPAA) and Personal Health Information (PHI). When we talk about ethics and ethical behavior, we are never far away from the important concepts discussed in the following text.

ETHICS DEMYSTIFIED

The NASW *Code of Ethics* can be a bit overwhelming for both experienced and novice social workers. In their book *Delivering Health Care in America: A Systems Approach*, Shi and Singh do an excellent job of looking at the basic elements.

Shi and Singh refer to four principles that may help you understand this important issue: respect for others, beneficence, non-maleficence, and justice. Respect for others has four subcomponents: autonomy, truth-telling, confidentiality, and fidelity. First, autonomy refers to the client's right to make decisions for himself or herself, meaning the client is a partner in the planning of treatment, by giving his or her consent and making choices without coercion. If you have ever been a patient in a hospital, you will understand how patients often feel they are at the mercy of the caregivers. This is an area where professionals often have difficulty; they feel they are the experts and neglect to include clients in treatment decisions. Next, we have truth-telling, which simply means that you are honest with your client. If your client asks questions and you don't know the answers, don't guess, but try to find the answer. Faking the answer will not foster a trusting relationship.

The third subcomponent is confidentiality of information; it is your duty to protect information about your client from third parties. Recently, in an article, Nancy McKenna (Update Vol. 34, No 4, 2010) spoke about being a school social worker and how "social workers cannot offer students complete confidentiality." She was quoting one of her sources, Kagle and Kopels. Rules change depending on the agency and the clientele you are serving. However, she raises an important question and concept: is the information you are sharing relevant either to helping your student either in the academic arena or to their social-emotional growth? Be sure to discuss HIPAA with your supervisor. However, you will often work as a team. When you are required to share with your supervisor information about your work, you may do so because then you would not be violating the HIPAA, (Health Information Portability and Accountability Act). The fourth component is fidelity, meaning you keep your word and always demonstrate professional behavior expected of the social work profession. This can refer to anything, from the time and day you will meet your client, rescheduling in advance when necessary, to keeping your word if you say you are going to fill out those forms or make that call. Also, introduce yourself as the social work student or social work intern to define your role and your duties; in fact, clarify your role in your first meeting with the client.

Beneficence simply means that, as you enter into the client-worker relationship, you undertake to do all you can to alleviate the client's pain and suffering. You may think this applies more to the medical profession, but there are all types of suffering. Going hand in hand with beneficence is non-maleficence. Simply put, *non-maleficence* means your moral obligation to do no harm. This is an issue not just for doctors but also for social workers and all helping professions. Your client interventions, group meetings, or meetings to develop programs all require the same level of professionalism from you. The concept of doing no harm equally applies to working with multiple agencies in a meeting. The final element of ethical behavior is justice. You should treat your client with fairness and be nondiscriminatory, which at times can be difficult.

You will find embedded in your agency code of ethics these simple but relevant four basic principles. They are to be valued and should be part of your values as a social worker.

SOCIAL WORK ETHICS

Values

More than likely, you were attracted to the field of social work at least partially because your personal values are the same as those of other social workers. Throughout its history, social work values have remained consistent. The *Code of Ethics* of the NASW is based on the six core values of social work:

- Service ("Social workers' primary goal is to help people in need and to address social problems.")
- Social justice ("Social workers challenge social injustice.")
- Dignity and worth of the person ("Social workers respect the inherent dignity and worth of the person.")
- Importance of human relationships ("Social workers recognize the central importance of human relationships.")
- Integrity ("Social workers behave in a trustworthy manner.")
- Competence ("Social workers practice within their areas of competence and develop and enhance their professional expertise.")

You may want to post these values above your desk or in a prominent place so they can inspire and inform you in your daily activities. It will be helpful to read and review these values often.

Within the NASW's *Code of Ethics* are many subcategories, resulting in a text of 22 pages. Reading the full text either as a class assignment or on your own, but know it is a daunting task. I will touch on some of the main points now.

Resources in Dealing with Ethical Issues

When you are faced with an ethical dilemma or uncertain about your course of action, many resources are available to help you. Of course, you should consult with your supervisor about any ethical dilemmas you experience. You may also want to discuss these issues with your peers and perhaps with selected coworkers, and often this is material for in-class discussions. It is possible that the students in the college discussion, in class, and in the agency see the situation differently. Do not get in the middle if this occurs; your faculty supervisor will take the lead if necessary.

1. NASW's *Code of Ethics*. You should already be very familiar with the social work code of ethics. Hopefully, you have studied and discussed it thoroughly with your professors. Now is your chance to put these principles to work on a daily basis. Keep a copy of the *Code of Ethics* handy so you can consult it whenever you have doubts about what you should and should not do. In keeping with today's world, you can go green and not print a copy of the 22 pages but instead be familiar with its location on NASW's website.

2. Another great resource for both you and your supervisor is the NASW Office of Ethics and Professional Review. As a student member of the NASW, you may consult by telephone with a representative of the NASW who can offer ethical advice via a toll-free line.

3. Additionally, NASW's website features an *ethical dilemma of the month*. In this feature, composites of members' ethical issues are posted, along with a response indicating which section or sections of the NASW's *Code of Ethics* may apply to the issue. Questions for thought and discussion are also posted in order to help you reach good ethical decisions.

4. Many textbooks and DVDs about ethics in social work are available. You can locate them online at any of the many book companies, for example, Barnes and Noble or Amazon.com.

5. Some states have websites, you should become familiar with resources that are available to you no matter where you will be doing your practicum and later where you plan to practice as a professional social worker.

ETHICS AND ETHICAL THINKING

You have discussed the code of ethics in your classroom work; I have given you an overview, but now, let's focus on how the code translates to the field. However, it is important that you also know if the agency where you are doing your placement has a code of ethics. Many agencies have a generic version that applies to all staff with the expectation that as a professional you may be held to a higher standard.

CONFIDENTIALITY ISSUES IN AGENCIES

Are you allowed to talk to other workers about a case, or can you speak to only certain individuals? Are you allowed to discuss your client with workers from another agency? If so, what is the policy? Do you need a release of information? Don't assume; ask!

Please don't talk about your clients in the hallways. You will hear such conversations all the time, but it is not a good practice.

In your practicum, you may encounter a variety of ethical dilemmas. When your clients have violated their probation, are you obligated to tell the parole officer, or is this information confidential? If your client has a history of setting fires and is ready for placement, will you be expected to downplay this history so as to avoid rejection from the new placement? If your client is underage and tells you about behaviors that may be dangerous, do you tell his or her parents? If your client is HIV positive and is engaging in unprotected sex with someone you may know, should you warn that individual? If your client tells you in conversation of a situation that suggests neglect or abuse, what do you do?

Each situation has its own ethical issues that demonstrate the concerns and rights of the individual you are working with, and the rights of others. Ethical situations can be a minefield; seek the support of your supervisor and stay on solid ground.

First, always treat your clients with respect and dignity. Second, demonstrate good social work values and ethical behavior by following the code of ethics. Third, review the agency code of ethics, which can be found in the policy and procedures manual of your agency. Fourth, when in doubt, go to your supervisor or someone in the agency who can help. Do not act on your own without consultation from an authoritative source. Remember that you too have rights, values, and ethical standards that may also come into play in any ethical situation. Your personal rights and values may collide with your agency's policies or assignments. What happens when you do not agree with what you are told? Again, seek support from your supervisor and request that your field faculty guide you.

As a student social worker, you have ethical responsibilities, to clients, to colleagues of all disciplines, to the social work profession, and to society as a whole.

To Clients

Remember that you are your clients' advocate, and that you must treat each client (and family) with the utmost respect. This statement equally applies to your work in a macro setting. Respect is not something that you can take; it must be given to you by others. Earning respect is easy when you act professionally and respectfully. The key is to remember that your interactions with clients constitute a professional relationship.

Respect must be extended not only to the client, but also to your written work and when talking with colleagues about a client. If you have problems respecting a particular client, discuss the matter with your supervisor, since attitudes you may think are hidden could leak out in your speech, manner, or bearing. If you have conflicts with a client, this issue becomes important material for supervisory sessions.

Client is broad term that can be defined as an individual person, a group or family, an agency, or a group of agencies. Your placement and your supervisors will guide you on this path. Your client needs to be a partner in the process. Too often professionals act as if the client is not part of the process and perceive themselves as knowing what is best for the client. This failure to utilize the self-determination of a client is a critical error.

Confidentiality

One of the most important ethical issues regarding clients has to do with confidentiality. When do you discuss clients' rights and issues of confidentiality with your clients? Do you introduce the subject in the beginning when you first meet clients, and are you knowledgeable enough to discuss it with your clients at this point in your learning experience? What will happen if you explain it poorly? Will the clients trust you? And are you then put in a situation where you feel you need to share information with others but are not sure you explained the policy correctly to your clients?

As of April 14, 2003, we were all learning the ins and outs of the new Health Information Portability and Accountability Act, better known as HIPAA. This act, designed to create greater accountability on the part of providers of health services, has had an important impact on the providers of services and you as a social worker. This law affects everything from faxes sent to letters mailed that contain a client's health information. The agency where you are doing your practicum would be addressing the new HIPAA law and will explain to you its guidelines. There are some broad issues we will discuss now. First is the concept of *Protected Health Information*. Basically, any piece of information about a client that is considered confidential falls under this concept. You will see letters and packets labeled *PHI confidential* to be opened by the addressee only. In the past, a common way to send client information would be to write *confidential* on the envelope. The important thing to remember is that client information is confidential and as such it needs to be protected. The agency where you are doing your placement will show you the guidelines used by them. The second general issue is that of disclosures of information. The agency has a responsibility to track all disclosures of information for each client. This is often done on a form kept in the client record. What is or is not a disclosure needs to be discussed and also clarified by your agency. Take notes; don't just rely on your memory when you discuss this topic.

Your placement agency may give you more information on this topic and you will need it; always, ask for help from your supervisor if you don't understand something.

You can access more information from the web on this topic and you have already been exposed to HIPAA policy at your drug store and doctor's office. You may not realize it but one of the forms you signed was directly related to this policy. Be proactive and get a copy of the HIPAA policy handed out at your agency.

So with this new information, let's see how a student handles the topic of confidentiality in her process recording (see Table 2.1):

The dialogue shown in the table is a good example of a student's dilemma. The student is being exposed to the topic of confidentiality in the classroom and at the same time at his or her practicum. The student had no place to go but put the issue on the table with the patient as best as she could. Be aware there are many pressures on you to perform.

The written institutional procedures to protect clients' rights to confidentiality should be at your work location in a policy manual. Ask to see the manual even if you feel the supervisor has explained confidentiality and you feel you have a full and complete understanding of the concept and how it works. Do not think you know the agency's policies because of personal experience or because you have read your discipline's code of ethics. Each agency has its own rules concerning confidentiality. If these rules are not spelled out clearly in the agency manual, then ask for clarity on the subject from your agency supports, generally your supervisor.

Many agencies work in a team structure where information about clients is shared with all members of the team. This setup creates a more complex situation concerning

TABLE 2.1 Students' first attempt discussing confidentiality

He Said/She Said	Supervisor Comments
W: I want to go over confidentiality; do you know what that means?	
D: Yeah. You can't take my chart or information without my permission.	
W: Yes, there is more. What you say stays between me and you, unless you are going to harm yourself or others. I am obligated to tell my supervisor. (I wasn't sure. . . .)	Not really true, you tell all in this process recording.

what can and should be shared. Information shared can range from broad strokes about a client's life to specific and detailed situations.

If you work in an agency that treats clients under medication, is it your responsibility to share information with doctors so they can give the best possible care? Who has access to the client's records and how and from where is the information collected?

A client of mine reported that he was thinking about starting to drink again, and he was concerned because drinking had gotten him into a lot of trouble in the past. He also told me he lay awake at night and imagined having a sexual relationship with an attractive female in his therapy group.

What was important to share with a team was the concern that the client was considering drinking again and the impact that action may have had for that person. Relevant information, such as other members of the team interacting with this client, needs to be given. If you feel there is any danger to another client or the community, then you need to talk with the team, and know your agency's policies along with your state's laws concerning warning a person in danger.

Remember to discriminate between what is interesting or of shock value from what is actually important.

In team meeting one day, I observed that a male client had started plucking his eyebrows. Immediately following the meeting, a team member confronted the client, backing him against a wall and demanding to know if he was a homosexual or not. The client became agitated, upset, and seemed to be doing poorly for several weeks. From that time on, I was more careful about the kinds of information I relayed to that particular member of the team.

A simple rule of thumb will help: will the issue or event you are planning to disclose help the client in some way? Help should not be something relating necessarily to positives alone, but may include negatives as well. For example, telling someone that your client is drinking a six-pack of beer a day is a negative disclosure, but without that information, medications may be impacted and treatment providers will not be directed to the true picture.

A seasoned social worker reported to me that her client told her he had used drugs one time recently. He was under court-ordered drug treatment and if she disclosed this information the court would certainly have put him in jail. She did not want to report the one-time event because he had been doing so well before the slip. However, she knew that if she did not report the event to the court and there was another slip, they would want to be aware that this slip has happened before and thus establish a pattern. It was an unpopular disclosure but you can see why it was necessary. It may have hurt the client because he did go to jail but perhaps in the long run it saved him.

What if your client is an agency? How can you tell the boundaries of confidentiality? Does not everyone at the agency have the same status when it comes to confidentiality? As earlier discussed, McKenna raises the question: is what you are sharing relevant? Committees have many different roles and tasks; would sharing information from your meeting be useful or could it result in misunderstanding? Discuss this issue with your supervisor and get his or her guidance. You will be expected to share information about situations such as what occurred at a committee meeting or a planning group and there will be other times when you may be expected to not disclose the information gathered.

My student began her day attending the hospital-wide rounds. Representatives from many disciplines, departments, and various programs discussed issues related to the patient population over the past twenty-four hours. She quickly became aware that she was now privileged to a wealth of confidential information. Now her task was to judge what was relevant to share and with whom, as she was given follow-up assignments.

The Internet

When we discuss ethical concerns on the Internet, microblogging (e.g., Twitter), social networking (e.g., MySpace), text messaging, and email must be discussed. As these forms of communication have become part of our lives, we rarely think of the power these forms of communication can have. We recognize the risks when, for example, TV networks publicize a tragic death and points to cyber-bullying as the cause. The Internet is a normal part of our lives but client confidentiality is not to be taken lightly. Be very careful about what you are sharing with the world outside about your agency. Never give out any information that can identify a client or even a staff member. Names, I am sure you understand, are among the identifying information but the latter also includes descriptions or characteristics of a person that would identify him or her. It is best to avoid putting anything on the web; there are too many risks. Some agencies have their own email systems that are encrypted with firewall applications to protect the system; others rely on a server on the web for communication. These open systems are at high risk. Closed systems with firewall applications still have agency policies about client confidentiality.

Access to Records

Due to the changes in various state and federal laws, clients now have greater access to their personal records than ever before. Be informed about the laws in your state, and ask your supervisor about your responsibilities in making records available to clients. Without going into great detail, you should be aware that rules change depending on the source of the information. For example, access to records from agencies for the treatment of drugs and alcohol often have their own forms for disclosure, whereas you will find a different procedure for agencies providing psychiatric treatment. But let's not stop here; when we talk about records involving children, releasing records can all be an entirely different process. And not to be outdone, there are very strict rules when we are discussing AIDS and HIV. This consumer access could influence what you might write in progress reports or chart notes. In our discussion of ethical concerns, I reminded you that a case record is a legal document. The record should reflect only the client and not any other agenda. You should never read in a client's chart information such as social worker Jane is out on extended leave due to breast cancer and you are now the social worker for this client. Let me regress here for a minute. Remember our discussion about reporting information that is relevant and screening out the rest. That applies to conversations but also to your note writing. You have an ethical responsibility to report information accurately and professionally.

Relationships

Professional boundaries are the key to understanding a relationship. Often, those professional boundaries are tested; being clear on your professional role will guide you.

Sexual relationships with current or former clients are unethical. In addition, the *Code of Ethics* states, (NASW Code Of Ethics, p. 13) "Providing clinical services to a former sexual partner has the potential to be harmful to the individual and is likely to make it difficult for the social worker and individual to maintain appropriate professional boundaries." Be sure you know both the *Code*'s material relating to appropriate physical contact with clients and clear boundary setting. Of course, any form of sexual harassment is off limits.

Social relationships with clients or clients' family members are also not permitted. If you live in a small town, for example, there may be sticky issues involved if you already know the client even slightly or attend the same school, church, or synagogue. Additionally, if you keep bumping into a client, that can be uncomfortable for you as well as for your client. Check with your supervisor for his or her expectations in this regard. Will you be expected to pretend you don't know your client if you accidentally meet him or her in a social situation? At what point will you be expected to speak up and tell your supervisor that you cannot work with a particular client because you are too close to that person to be objective?

Family Contact and Confidentiality

In conjunction with knowing your client's health issues, you will need to know under what circumstance those issues, and other client issues, can be released to or discussed with others. It is especially critical to know what you can and cannot discuss with the client's family members. First, get to know the agency policy concerning contact with families. The rules of confidentiality in the medical field have been getting a good deal of attention recently, with the passage of HIPAA. HIPAA is a federal law that provides for the transfer of insurance benefits when changing employers or insurance companies. This has impacted the rules covering confidentiality because in order to efficiently transfer insurance coverage the companies need to efficiently exchange medical information. HIPAA defines what information can be exchanged with and without consent and how it can be exchanged. Despite the passing of this federal law, there is a great deal of difference in how individual agencies have interpreted its guidelines. You must check with your supervisor to determine what your agency policy is and how it is to be carried out.

Ethical Behavior toward Colleagues

Ask—don't assume you already know the answer. Remember—the only dumb questions are the ones you didn't ask.

What does it mean to behave ethically toward colleagues? The concept of respect is paramount. Use the golden rule: treat your coworkers as you would like to be treated. This means no gossip, no backbiting, and so on. Make an honest effort to cooperate and be a good team member, even though you may not like or even respect all your colleagues. Remember that you have come from an idealistic perspective into the real world, which you may find to be different from you expected it to be. You may find that you question the maturity and ethical behavior of some of your colleagues when they do not behave perfectly. Remember that everyone is human, and we all have our bad days. Some of us have personal or professional problems that creep into dealings with others. It will be helpful if you can give your colleagues the benefit of the doubt and interpret their behavior in the most positive light possible.

In terms of the decision-making process, the ethical issues you will confront in the field are not that different from those that wind up with the ethics committee of your university. You will find in the general-hospital setting the ethics committee will meet as necessary, often dealing with life-and-death issues. Other institutions have monthly or even bi-monthly meetings. Membership can and should include a wide range of professional disciplines and laypersons. You will find this varies from agency to agency. Some agencies are very small and do not have the support of an ethics committee to bounce issues off; you are still bound by the code of ethics of your discipline. If you feel you are in an ethical dilemma, ask your supervisor what the procedure is to deal with the issue.

Recently, a student approached me very concerned with the events that had taken place at his agency relating to his client. This was a small agency that very often dealt with the court system. In this situation, there was no ethics committee but the matter was discussed in supervision without resolution. The ethical dilemma may be good material for great classroom discussion; however, there was no resolution for the student; but his persistence to bring the matter forward improved the agency as a whole and reinforced the importance of using your facility supervisor.

Not all ethical situations will be resolved to your satisfaction and you may be left with many confusing feelings. It is important to share this with your supervisor and your program director or coordinator. You need to process the feelings and grow from the experience.

Below is an approach to an ethical dilemma that highlights points you will need to address. You can find in any generalist book on social work some form of this outline.

Ethical Decision-Making Process

- Write down the ethical problem/issue.
- Who are involved? Make a list; think at micro, mezzo, and macro levels.
- Review ethical standards: do the issues present an ethical dilemma?
- Present the ethical dilemma to the treatment team, supervisor, or others; include your role/investment.
- Reevaluate the situation for degree of ethical issue. Continue or disengage discussion.
- What is your conclusion? (Does your supervisor support your decision?)

NOTES

NOTES

CHAPTER 3

Beginning at the Beginning

EMOTIONAL READINESS: "STANDING IN THE RAIN"

You can study the physical and chemical properties of rain. You can measure its impact on the environment. You can possess an intimate book-knowledge of rain down to its molecules. But what does it feel like to stand in the rain and feel the drops on your face?

In the same manner, you learn social work theories and techniques in the classroom; you read and discuss; you role-play; you study the research literature; and you test your knowledge. You have an intimate book-knowledge of social work, but what does it feel like to be a social worker?

Most students will make every effort to look and sound ready for their placement. They will often buy new clothing and evaluate their current wardrobe to make sure it looks professional. But you and I know that your quaking inner world may not match your confident exterior. Most students will tell you they feel unprepared for their first day, and they may even say they feel vulnerable, helpless, and even stupid in their new settings.

These feelings are all natural and normal. When you begin a whole new level of learning (which field work certainly is), you tend to regress back to earlier emotional states. It is not unusual to panic and feel like you're a three-year-old, even with a supportive supervisor and many people surrounding you reminding you, "You can do it—you have what it takes."

Remember: There will be new emotional pressures any time you learn, grow, or expose yourself to a new environment, no matter how much support you have. So, don't underestimate the impact your new placement will have on you.

When I began to write this book, I interviewed many students about their beginning field work experiences. I also talked to new and experienced social workers in various stages of their careers. I found similar feelings among undergraduate juniors preparing to enter their first field placement and seniors beginning their second placement. What may surprise you is that I heard the same feelings expressed by graduate students, social workers beginning their first jobs, and even seasoned workers who have changed settings or experienced changes in the structure of their work.

For example, one student talked about how intensely he prepared for his first internship by talking to the student who had just completed his field work at the same setting. They discussed in detail the agency staff, the clients served, and even the particular clients who would be assigned to the new student. Even with all this prior knowledge, the new student's experience was quite different from that of the student who just left.

Another social work student did all the homework she could, investigating the agency and its funding sources and speaking to two former students who were placed at that agency about its clients and the work. Halfway through the year, she noted how unprepared she felt for what she actually experienced in the field.

You wonder how, if these students had indeed done their homework as this book suggests and per their college professors' instructions, is it possible that they still felt so unprepared? The answer is simple: the preparatory activities the students did were intellectual, and their experiences in the field were loaded with emotional content. It is not a coincidence that you are here. You chose this path for reasons perhaps known only to you, but the fact that you are here still remains, having struggled through policy courses, research, and countless theories. You are ready for this phase of your development and the right to passage begins now.

"Standing in the rain" or beginning a field work practicum is a totally new experience. Its first effect on you will be to make you feel inadequate and ill-prepared. That's not at all true; but the flooding of emotions leads you to believe you're not up to the new challenges. Just take a deep breath, and remind yourself not to feel any of the things stated earlier. You are simply in another universe called field work agency placement. Welcome to all the new experiences and feelings. Your comfort zone has been the classroom as you are well experienced at being a student; now it is time to leave that comfortable place and start your practicum. Can you believe that I called being a student *being in a comfort zone?* Think back to the time when you started college and how you felt then. Were you relaxed or a bit anxious of the newness of college? You survived that and got past that time to where you are now; this is just a new beginning.

A student came to class reporting how much she enjoyed her placement and how great it was that she could do intake assessments on all the new clients. She was feeling very comfortable with the placement, not realizing she was doing a task she was very familiar with from her previous job. Regardless of why her supervisor allowed this situation to happen, it is more important you understand the problem from the student's perspective. We all gravitate toward activities that are comfortable to us, so in this case the student was doing nothing wrong. However, the student was not being given tasks that were new and unfamiliar to her. This kind of situation is a disservice to the student, who needs to experience new learning situations that will probably be more uncomfortable than familiar ones.

If you're a student returning to school or beginning a second or even third career, you may feel that it will be easier for you to stand in the rain. Actually, this metaphor may apply to you even more than to the average student because you're taking backward steps in putting yourself in a one-down position after you've been accustomed to a higher rung on the career ladder.

One final note about emotional readiness: you will never be fully prepared for what is to come. You will never have all the confidence or the information you want and need. That's life. What's important to remember is that your feelings are natural and normal and that you can still move forward and learn what you need to learn despite your fears and negative emotions.

You have discussed in the classroom the importance of recognizing your feeling when you are working with clients and, as you know, there is a column on your process recording to put down on paper your feeling and even your analysis of your thoughts and feelings. Here is your first opportunity to look at your feeling and perform self-analysis, before you speak to a client.

THE FIRST DAY

The first few days of field work placement can be harrowing because you may be keyed up and nervous with anticipation, unsure of yourself, self-conscious, and doubting your ability to measure up to set standards. And because you are so excited and anxious, you may not even have had enough sleep. All these factors make a new situation seem daunting. Some general tips for navigating a new beginning are discussed later.

Most of this information has been covered, but a quick reminder follows. Get as much information as you can about your placement, the clients, the supervisor, and your coworkers ahead of time. Talk to others who have been at the same agency before you. The more detailed information you have before the first day, the more prepared you will feel.

Give yourself some time to understand the political environment. Observe quietly, and notice who is aligned with whom, where the real power lies, and who's wearing the black hats and white hats. Be particularly observant in meetings to get a feel for what's going on. Be friendly with everyone, but not overly familiar. You may feel lonely and out of place, but don't align quickly with anyone until you get a feel for the political climate. If, for example, you become chummy with someone who doesn't get along with your supervisor, you could be borrowing trouble. Don't allow yourself to get cornered by a coworker with a hidden or not-so-hidden agenda. Listen more than you talk. Be ready for agency staff to ask questions that may put you on the spot.

It was my first day at the agency. At the end of my first staff meeting, someone asked me what I thought of my placement after the first day. I said I could see that the staff worked well as a team, and I was sure I would get a lot out of my field work here. Half kidding and half seriously, the medical director turned to another coworker and laughed. "Well, we fooled another one, didn't we?" I felt a little foolish for answering such a dangerous question. It was only weeks later that I began to see how the staff climate was very tense, with workers feeling hostile and angry with one another because of unequal workloads.

Earn your *idiosyncrasy credit* by keeping a low profile for a while. Fit in with the way things are done; be quiet and cooperative; *play the game* as you understand it; and make an honest effort to do what seems to be expected of you. After you've been around for a while, your coworkers will trust and respect you more, and you will have earned the right to have your own opinions and personal style. You will be allowed to be *yourself*, a unique individual. As discussed earlier here are some don'ts: Don't wear loud or unusual clothing; don't talk about yourself, your personal problems, your boyfriend/girlfriend, your weekends, your private life; and don't gossip. Your differences will be more likely to be tolerated after your coworkers gotten to know and trust you than at the very beginning. Then you'll be seen as one of us.

Don't set things up so you have to be reminded to be somewhere at a certain time by your supervisor. Be "clock conscious" and plan ahead to get there on your own.

Be punctual. Better to be a little early than late. Tardiness might be interpreted as laziness, lack of interest, lack of planning, or disorganization. Think ahead and make extra special efforts to be where you're supposed to be on time.

Listen and be attentive at meetings. If unfamiliar terms or abbreviations are used, write them down so you can look them up later. Perhaps you can ask your peers or your supervisor at a later time. If you ask elementary questions at a meeting, you may seem unprepared. As you get more comfortable over time, you'll feel more comfortable taking risks in asking questions, or making tentative interpretations.

Unless you already know where everyone sits at meetings, wait until most people are seated, or find a place at the back. You may accidentally sit in someone's favorite chair. If you are asked to come forward, that's fine, but it might be embarrassing to be told you're too forward.

Be humble. Acknowledge your lack of experience and training. Remember, you're an intern, not a seasoned professional. It's OK to be unsure of yourself, but it's not OK to pretend to be more confident than you really are. Some students try to cover up their anxieties and insecurities with false bluster. The supervisor and coworkers will more readily respect true humility than grandiose overconfidence. Humility demonstrates that you're teachable and cooperative, whereas the person who comes in with a know-it-all attitude can be a real pain.

A student began his practicum at a prestigious agency and the director, though new, was also from a distinguished training institute. When the student came to supervision, there was an unexpected surprise for the supervisor. The student informed his supervisor that the treatment design of the program was not a design that he agreed with as an approach to treatment.

Needless to say, why would a student begin supervision with this statement? I am telling you to be humble, to listen, and to learn not be bold and attacking. Yes, the year was long and difficult for the student.

Quick tip: If you're really nervous and your hands are shaking, you might want to pass on the soft drink or cup of coffee that's offered to you. It wouldn't be the end of the world if you spilled it all over yourself or someone else, but why take the chance?

How do you get good judgment? Good judgment comes only with experience. How do you get experience? Experience comes from making mistakes. Learn that your mistakes will help you mature in your skills as a social worker.

UNDERSTANDING YOUR CLIENT (STARTING WHERE THE CLIENT IS)

If social work was a building and we were to name the cornerstones, one would surely be the phrase, "Start where the client is." This phrase sounds simple, but it can be very complicated even for a seasoned professional.

A Student's First Steps

He Said/She Said	Supervisor Comments
W: Hi D.	
H: Hi.	
W: I'll be your social worker. I'm a student. (Feels comfortable speaking to him.)	
D: You're not a worker?	Sounds like the client is concerned with your qualifications.
W: No, I am a social work intern; I'll be here until May.	Good comeback.
D: OK.	
W: I want to go over confidentiality; do you know what that means?	Why did we start here, rather than where the client is.

This process recording has a number of items but let's focus on the topic of knowing what the client's issue is. Here, we see a student worried about getting in all the important things she was taught, especially issues of confidentiality. She did not give the client time to express why he was there. The student's qualifications were questioned as well, but this was not addressed by the student. These are common mistakes that students will make early in their placement, anxious to do a good job and say all the right things.

A Student Wants It Perfect

He Said/She Said	Supervisor Comments
W: Good morning! Thank you for meeting with me.	
C: (almost inaudible) Good morning!	
W: I guess I'll start by telling you about my role here.	
C: (nod) (I don't know what to say. I wanted to say the perfect thing to draw her out, knowing that it wasn't possible.)	
W: I am a social work student and that basically means that I have more time to meet with you because I have fewer clients. Have you ever worked with a student before?	Stop after who you are. This is true but would she care? What does it mean to her?
C: Yes. (I felt uncomfortable.)	Closed question

It is important that the client understands who you are and your role; therefore, you must be clear about your role in the placement. This student demonstrated a clear understanding of her role. The next process recording is that of a student's first client on week one of the placement.

Students with Sweating Palms

He Said/She Said	Supervisor Comments
W: What movie are you watching?	
C: It's about Vikings, I don't know much about Vikings.	
W: Me neither. so you like movies with war in them?	Assume
C: Yeah. (Start slow, maybe he doesn't want to speak.)	Closed question.
W: So are you hot?	Closed question.
C: No, I'm fine. It's cold outside.	
W: Yeah, it is really gloomy out today. Are you enjoying the MICA meetings?	Topic change here
(Starting to sweat a little; maybe I should say you're sweating, but I think that would have put him deeper in his shell.)	So many topics: heat, weather, groups. Take a deep breath, slow down. I think you're sweating?

The Rule of Three applies to many situations in life. The first third of clients can sit down and express their needs and goals with little difficulty. These clients may change along the way, but basically they remain constant from start to finish.

The second third have difficulty expressing their needs and they may change significantly before the end of treatment. What the first two groups have in common is that they have the capacity to express their needs.

As you have already guessed, the last third of clients lack the capacity to identify their own needs and issues. This is where you as their social worker need to help your clients to identify their needs. Read further for an example.

Client and Student on First Day

He Said/She Said	Supervisor Comments
W: Hi, I'm going to meet with you every Tue, at 1:00 PM. Do you remember my name?	We discussed; don't put the client on defense.
C: No.	
W: My name is…. (Intro could've been better, I could have said I'm a student, I'm nervous.)	
C: What are we going to talk about?	
W: Anything you want to talk about, for example, how your day is going	Closed question. Look for open-ended questions.
C: Good.	
W: How long have you been coming here?	Closed.
C: A while.	
W: Do you enjoy it here?	Closed.
C: Yes.	

The student found herself with the problem of closed-ended questions. It is much easier to think of open-ended questions in the classroom with your peers than with a client. It takes time to feel relaxed so you can ask better questions. Part of the problem is not the questions; it is the responses. In conversations, we often ask closed-ended questions, but the person we are speaking with gives us more than a *yes* or *no*.

With this group of clients, who can't express their needs and issues, you need to do two things: You need to feed them today so that you will be able to teach them to fish tomorrow to fend for themselves for much of their lives.

Whatever situation the client presents must be addressed, even if it truly seems unrelated to the client's goals and needs. So you must start with feeding the client in the situation that he or she is in, and that may be far from where you think the client should be. But the client cannot move past the current situation until his or her initial concerns—however trivial or senseless they seem to be—are addressed in the session.

At this point, it really does not matter what you think is good for the client, since you don't know yet what the client's goals are. This is just like how you can't really think about an upcoming test for abnormal psychology until you've eaten your lunch. If you're starving, you will be internally distracted until you get your hunger taken care of.

I was having so many problems at home that I could not concentrate on my internship. I was not sleeping well and was stressed all the time. I needed the family problems to get settled before I could really concentrate and hear what my supervisor was trying to teach me. Thank goodness, he understood and helped me by not moving too fast. I guess he was starting with me from where I was.

Now the second part becomes clear. You can begin to work on the issues and goals of the client once you have passed this hurdle, and so you can teach the client to fish.

A supervisor said, "I have a client in my private practice who has never made it past the need to be fed." Without going into all the dynamics of the case, this individual comes in always in need of being fed, at which point she does not come back for several weeks, until the next crisis in her life. Because of her style of dealing with the treatment, she has not learned to fish. Perhaps one day she will be able to move past this point, but until then, the task of the social worker is to go at the pace the client sets.

OPEN-ENDED QUESTIONS

How many times have you been taught to ask open-ended questions, instead of questions that can be answered with a one-word answer? These are questions that draw out clients and help them feel relaxed with you so they can think out loud. Even though you have role-played countless times with your peers, when you begin your field work, you may often find yourself in a situation where it feels like "pulling teeth" in order to get any useful information from clients. Thinking on your feet is a lot harder than thinking in practice situations, and it takes time to get the hang of it.

You will not be the first or last student to become the victim of the closed-ended question. Some clients are extremely verbal and when asked a question, closed or not, they will give you a wealth of information. Here, you may wish for shorter answers and you may look for ways to contain the amount of information. Some clients will only answer the question. You will need to learn ways to gather your information and avoid those short answers such as *yes*, *no*, and *good*. Remember, there are two people in the room. How is the client feeling about the dialogue?

How is the client feeling, sitting in this room with you? How are you feeling? Each time you meet with your client, there is a process that starts when you come together and ends when you terminate the meeting. This is a chain that connects all your meetings with the client. It does not matter if you are to meet with the client three times or for three months, the chain still exists. What is the goal of the first meeting? What are the client's issues and what is the client's expectation of what you and the agency have to offer? There are two things to be kept in mind. First, you must establish a working relationship with your client and a rapport. Second, you must always begin your meeting with the client at the situation in which he or she is at that moment.

So go ahead, ask those closed-ended questions; but then analyze your own work and see how you can improve. Each client meeting is an opportunity to learn and grow as a professional social worker.

SOME FIRST MEETING PROCESS RECORDINGS

Process recording 1:

Purpose of the contact: This is the first meeting with the client. She is requesting counseling. My main goal is to establish rapport with the client.

Basic Client Description: The client is a young adolescent; she is the middle child of three children. Her parents have been divorced for a number of years and she lives with her father. She feels depressed at times and is requesting counseling to help her cope with these feelings.

A Student in a Hurry: A Case of Nerves

Dialogue	Supervisor Comments
Student: Hi, I am Sara.... You are ...? Get seated in room.	"I read your intake form and you tell me in your own words why you are here?"
Student: Can you tell me a little about yourself? (Feeling really nervous.)	
Client: Well I play these two sports . . . and I like . . . and I like. . . .	
(Not what I had in mind but OK. Perhaps I should have asked what her reason for coming here was.)	Good pick up. What could you have done differently?
Student: Is there anything you want to talk about? Anything bothering you?	
Client: My parents are divorced and I get depressed.	
(Why is she not telling me all of it? I know there is more.)	Don't rush!
(I feel like I am talking to a friend; drama.)	Careful! Maintain your professional boundaries.

What you see in this process recording is a student getting her sea legs, as they say. She is caught in the struggle to get past her own feelings. Does this first meeting go better as they move further into the meeting? Here are some of the student's comments later in the meeting: "I feel so useless being in the room. What else can I say?" and "It hasn't even been ten minutes yet. . . . I am sure we will end soon."

In the next situation, the student must complete a standardized form of this agency; it is their version of a psycho-social—talk about closed-ended questions. The agency runs an adult protective program; they need very specific information for their paperwork trail.

Dialogue	Supervisor Comments
Student: Hi, I am Sam. Do you remember we were to meet at 10:00? (Feeling nervous.)	What if he did not remember? Is there a better way to start?
Client: Oh yes.	
Student: How are you doing?	Closed question.
Client: Good.	
Student: Can you tell me a little about yourself? (I feel calm; we are in a conversation.)	Good question. It's open ended. But does the client know why you are there?

This student may question if this career choice is the right path after this encounter. You can see that closed-ended questions can result in feeling like you are pulling teeth. Try to ask the question again but this time make it open ended. You may be surprised.

A Student Goes to Dental School

He Said/She Said	Supervisor Comments
(Client is waiting to see me; I felt a little excited about today.)	
W: Do you know my name?	What made you ask this question?
C: No.	
W: My name is….	
C: Oh.	What do you know about the housing she lives in?
(It's like pulling teeth!)	
W: So, did you have a nice weekend?	
C: Yes.	
W: What did you do?	
C: Just sit. . . .	
(. . . Searching for a lead in question.)	
W: Just sit, did you go anywhere?	Good try, is she going to let you in?
C: No, just sit around.	
W: Did other people at the house go somewhere?	
C: No, they sat around.	

GETTING COMFORTABLE WITH YOUR CLIENTS

Deep listening means that you are fully present with your client. You are concentrating on both the content of what is being said, as well as the underlying feelings. Deep listening is a way of listening *with the heart* and with understanding and empathy. You are not rehearsing what you are going to say next; you are simply getting a feel of what your client's emotional and mental worlds are like.

This is a simple example of a session with a client where the student felt comfortable exploring new material.

A Student Feels Stupid

He Said/She Said	Supervisor Comments
W: Not to switch subjects, but last week you spoke about your wife. I was wondering what made you get married at a young age. You were 21 and she was 19.	You need to close an old topic before changing to a new one.
(I wanted to get to know him more, more than just about his goals, who he was before his illness.)	
C: No, I was 19 and she was 21.	
W: Oh, that's right you were younger than her.	
(I felt stupid because I forgot he told me.)	You are allowed to be human
C: I was smoking a lot of reefer and I met her at her sister's house. I smoked with her.	"Her" meaning the sister?
W: So you got married because you were on drugs?	
C: I can't say that.	
W: So it was a common bond between you and her?	Was she using drugs? Did she think he would stop?
(Was that judgmental? I didn't mean to it to be.)	

These process recordings are examples of common situations students get themselves into early in their placement.

A Professional Student

He Said/She Said	Supervisor Comments
C: When I first came here, the doctors said I was schizophrenic. I don't know if that was caused by smoking marijuana. What are you? A psychologist? A psychiatrist? (Confused on why he got that assessment.)	
W: No, I'm a social work student but I can tell you what schizophrenia is. (He is looking interested. Nervous, I didn't want to mess up.)	Sounds very professional; put in layperson terms.
C: OK.	
W: Schizophrenia is a disorder of the brain, the symptoms include..............................	

Don't get stuck in professional jargon. Don't talk down to your clients or above their heads. If in doubt, ask your clients if they understand and ask them to explain concepts back to you in their own words.

A Born Leader

He Said/She Said	Supervisor Comments
W: It must be frustrating for you.	Leading.
C: Yes, I was just talking about that to a friend of mine. I should be working or doing something now.	He got you hook line and sinker.
W: It sounds like you are a little down	Leading.
C: Sometimes I am; but I am working hard to change that.	There is a difference—asking a feeling question to get validation.
W: You are working hard to change. (Felt sad for him. Felt like I wanted to fix everything for him. I was trying to tune into him.)	

Trust your feelings: if you sense a client is feeling a certain way, ask! Don't fill in the blank for the client; you could be wrong. If you find your client is struggling for a word, provide suggestions and choices. For example, you may ask, "Are you feeling sad or blue or something else?"

An Anxious Student

He Said/She Said	Supervisor Comments
W: Before we stop and you make your call home, I want to ask you something.	Feeling unsure as to how things are going.
C: OK, I can make my phone call after that.	He will say anything to use the phone at this moment.
W: Yes. I want to ask: did you like the session that you and I had?	
C: Yes.	
W: Are there any topics that you would like to focus on?	This is where you begin the session.

STUDENT SAFETY

If you are endangered, who has the power to help you out of trouble? You may be surprised to learn that at many agencies, the level of safety has a great deal to do with workers helping one another. For example, a janitor or secretary may have a rapport with clients and be able to step in and "rescue" you from a difficult situation. For this reason, take pains to make friends with all the staff, not just the professionals. Chat with them; ask about their families; and don't think you're better than they are just because you've been to college and they haven't. Some workers resent students who give the appearance of acting superior to others. The truth is that often these students don't feel superior at all, but are ill-at-ease, shy, or unsure of themselves and often come off as arrogant. Make sure no one gets that impression of you, and when you're in a crunch, you may find help coming from unexpected sources.

A Student Survives a Surprise

He Said/She Said	Supervisor Comments
W: You were in … hospital? How did you get to this hospital? Were you agitated with someone?	Very confrontational start!!!
(I read his chart and it said he was acting in a bizarre manner and irritated.)	
(He then started to yell and point at me. He turned his chair around and sat sideways.)	Address behavior.
C: You calling me crazy? Do you think I am psycho?	What did he hear you say?
W: I didn't say you were crazy.	
(I was a little nervous because I never had a client yell at me. I was trying not to be defensive but I made my point. I didn't mean to offend him.)	Good, be careful!
C: No, you implied it.	
W: How did I imply that?	
C: (starts to laugh.) Silence I need a beer.	
(He has a history of alcohol abuse. I ignored the last topic because it overwhelmed me; my anxiety levels were up.)	
W: When was the last time you had a beer?	Good question. Topic change; can tell you were re-grouping.

Can you imagine what this student must have been feeling at that time? She handled the situation nicely for a first-year intern. However, the importance of the process recording is that you often don't know when a situation will become threatening. Ideally, this client would never have been assigned to a student if there had been any indication this would happen.

The next process recording helps us recognize that things are not always as they appear.

Love Is in the Air, or Is It Cologne?

He Said/She Said	Student Feelings
W: Hi J how are you today?	I am feeling relaxed, having seen J several times before.
J: I am feeling really good.	He is showered and neatly dressed, seems different???
W: That's great can you tell me more?	Wondered why the sudden change.
J: Well I really don't want to talk about it.	Concerned he is hiding something. Based on his history it could be several things.
W: Why don't you want to talk? Is it something that you fell I will disapprove?	Is it that he is using drugs again? Don't know what to ask. Frustrated!
W: I smell some really nice. Are you wearing cologne?	
J: Yes, it is that brand you told me about several weeks ago.	
W: J, are you seeing someone?	Concerned. He has a history of stalking his last girl friend.
W: You remember what happed the last time you were seeing someone? (Silence)	
J: I don't want to talk about it. And it's time to leave and get to the program.	

As we discuss this process recording, note that the student explained how the boy had gotten in trouble with the law by stalking a teenage girl near his age. She was concerned that it was happening again and it needed to be addressed. I asked her to consider other possible reasons for this incident to have occurred, as an exercise in problem solving. She offered a number of other possibilities. It was a good exercise and she was able to see how this technique could help her develop new ways of looking at the same issue. I suggested the possibility that she was the woman in his life. When asked to consider this possibility, she dismissed it. One week later, this student charged into my office to tell me some news. That week, she arrived at the home early and the father reported that every time she is scheduled to visit, his son showers and puts on cologne. We could go on here and explore the reasons why he did that and discuss adolescent fantasies, but that is not the lesson here. The lesson here is to not underestimate your relationship with your client. In this case, the student's social work professionalism and her skills at maintaining therapeutic boundaries were important assets.

INNER CLOCK

The inner clock of the individual may not keep time the same way as your clock; therefore, you will need to learn how this affects your relationship with your client. Often, seasoned social workers will come into supervision and report a situation in which they feel annoyed or angry at their client.

A visual illustration will help you understand. If I were to ask you and your client to stand and turn in a circle, you would quickly see that the two of you would turn at different speeds. Only some of the time would you be face to face. You can try this with a friend to get the idea.

What this example shows is that people move at different rates. Such things as mental confusion due to stress, a traumatic event, or effects of medication could all result in an individual moving at a different rate than he or she usually normally would. Because of illness, trauma, medication, or various factors, his or her speed of thinking and moving may never again be the same for the rest of his or her life. We are always changed by the events in our lives and some of them cannot be undone. Please remember this about your clients and be compassionate in your expectations of them.

The point is that you may forget the individual is a client and that may affect his or her ability to communicate with you. So, as you are feeling the anxiety of your newness to the profession, it is hard not to fill every silence and every gap in the conversation. Waiting for the client to process information and respond to you can feel like an eternity. Please understand that all you are doing is waiting until they turn and face you, so to speak. There is an expression that "fools rush in where angels fear to tread"; so do social work students eager to help.

This point applies equally to group work and working with other agencies. Agencies are represented by individuals. So you have the agencies moving at different speeds and the individuals within the various agencies moving at different speeds. There is a lot going on in the room when you are working with different groups.

LEAVING SPACE

Leaving space means that when you ask a question or make a statement, you leave enough time for the client to reply to you. *Leaving space* may mean that you must exercise more patience than you ever have in your life.

Although we are discussing the issue of leaving space here in the beginning phase, you will probably not fully understand the concept until you are well into the middle phase of your placement. Why is it so hard to leave space? Well, remember how anxious you were feeling as a student doing your first interview. There is a lot going on in the room and it takes time to develop these skills. You ask what you think is an open-ended question, and you are eager to hear your client's response. How eager are you? Did you leave time for the client to answer? When I say "enough time," I mean by the client's clock, not your timetable.

Leaving space is a term that has to do with allowing time for your client to open up to you and respond. It has to do with your being able to tolerate silence and lack of immediate response on the part of your client. It seems so simple, and it looks like such a basic idea that you may think you should be able to leave space right from the beginning of your field work. You should know that leaving space is more difficult than it appears, and it has a great deal to do with your maturing skills. Don't get discouraged if you aren't able to master this skill immediately. As you develop this skill, you will suddenly realize you are not as anxious and can concentrate on learning more of the skills and techniques of being with your clients in an effective way. A student who realized she had finally learned how to leave space once said, "I did not feel rushed and I was not hurried to ask the next question." She realized that she was able to elicit a response with the same question she asked on day one, but the difference now was that she was able to hear the response more fully and get an answer that led her to ask new questions.

BECOMING THE LEAST MOTIVATED PERSON IN THE ROOM

Remember that your clients' goals are more important than your goals for a client. You may have a hidden or overt agenda for your client, and believe that he or she should accomplish a particular result on a particular timetable. You must remember, however, that your world is not your client's world, and what is important is for you to support your client in making healthy choices (even though he or she may not be in line with your values or expectations). You must realize that clients have their own inner clocks, which may not coincide with your sense of time.

When I was younger, I expected clients to have certain goals; I expected them to be taking orderly and logical steps to achieve them; and I expected them to take a minimum amount of time to get there. I wanted them all to have jobs, their own apartments, and good social skills. Imagine my frustration when my clients did not want the same things for themselves that I wanted for them. I was especially baffled when they seemed satisfied with lesser goals or were able to achieve goals by skipping steps I considered essential.

ASKING

A very common error students make in the first days of their placement is to assume they know what the client is meaning or feeling. You make these assumptions based on your own sets of values, and not your clients' values. You can guess correctly if the client shares your values; but too often, you can guess wrongly and then you are not helping your clients achieve their goals. In some ways, you are clueless as to what your client truly means by his or her statements. These assumptions may leave the client feeling that his or her meeting with you was useless, not helpful, or even destructive. Don't find yourself assuming things rather than asking questions to get clarity.

LEARNING TO TOLERATE AMBIGUITY AND AMBIVALENCE

As you are thrown into new situations and environments, you will find your inner world enlarging. At times, you may be overwhelmed or confused about all the contradictory data presented to you. You may find some of your most cherished beliefs are seen in a whole new light in view of what you are learning. You may find that at one point, X seems to be true, and yet at other times, Y also seems equally true even though they are totally opposite. You will find that you do not have all the answers and that you may need to unlearn some ideas you once held. As a result, field placement will be rich in challenges as you adjust to how you see the world in new ways.

If you are committed to never opening your mind to new possibilities or to never changing your ideas about something, you may be resisting new ideas. It can be difficult to deal with inner conflicts, but as you mature, you will learn to be more tolerant of the clash of opposing ideas without trying to oversimplify things so much that there is no more ambiguity.

As you mature as a social worker, you will also become more comfortable with your own ambivalence, as well as the ambivalence in your clients' thinking. We can have conflicting feelings about a given issue. You may love someone dearly, yet have feelings of irritation and be upset when there are conflicts. As you learn to accept your own divided emotions, you will be better able to tolerate the inner conflicts of your clients.

One of my clients was in a long-term relationship with an abusive boyfriend. She kept saying she was going to leave him, but at the same time, she really loved him and didn't want to live without him.

I had worked with her for several weeks, and was beginning to get very frustrated with her because she couldn't make up her mind and take the right actions. As I processed my feelings with my supervisor, she explained to me that my client was "sitting in the question," and was working through her ambivalence in her own way and in her own time. She also helped me to understand that my efforts to push her into what I thought she should do were not being helpful to her. In fact, I began to understand that by pushing in one direction, I was actually drawing out an opposite reaction in my client, and that was counterproductive.

LEARNING TO TRUST AND USE YOUR FEELINGS

Before you can trust or use your feelings in working with clients, you must first be aware of what your feelings and thoughts are. It may seem strange to state that you may not know what you are feeling in a particular situation, but if you are honest with yourself, you will admit that often there are levels of emotions that you were not aware of until you took time to delve deeper into them.

There are several ways to become more sensitive to your own emotions: You may want to write down various thoughts and feelings throughout your field placement. Journaling is one of the most important tools you can use to further your growth as a social worker. Your journal can serve as a log book to jog your memory about dates or incidents, a record of the concepts and skills you have learned, and your growing maturity as a human being. The more honest you can be in your journal about your mistakes and shortcomings, the more the journal can teach you about yourself and how you can interact effectively with your clients.

Fortunately, the profession of social work enhances and encourages your ability to become a fully functioning human being. As you encounter people who are different from and similar to you, you will gain more and more insight into your own behavior, feelings, and thoughts. You can also learn from the most negative of contacts with others, whether clients or coworkers.

As you become more and more aware of your own feelings and insights, you will want to check your perceptions with others to see how accurate those perceptions are. When you get a feeling or hunch about something, it will be helpful to see to what extent others validate your insights. Just because someone more experienced disagrees with you doesn't mean that person is right and you are wrong. You will benefit from an increasing openness in testing your reality with others. Over time, and with experience, you will naturally come to know that your feelings can be trusted.

PAYING ATTENTION TO YOUR BODY

As you learn to read your own emotions and bodily state, you will find that they are an enormous help in dealing with your clients. Listen to what your gut tells you. Does your stomach tighten up around certain people? Do you find yourself breathing more shallowly in some situations? What happens to your jaw muscles, your shoulders, your back? Where in your body do you tend to experience the emotions elicited in you by others?

For example, you may find yourself consistently getting angry or anxious with a particular client. Or you may find that you are suddenly sleepy and tired when dealing with another. These physical responses elicited by clients can be important clues in understanding their behavior. You may want to think about the strong possibility that the client often brings about the feelings he or she has in others in his or her environment.

If a client is often making the people in his or her life angry, then his or her experience of the world will be different from that of a client who does not elicit that anger in others.

I was assigned to work with a policeman at our agency. The problems he was discussing were not anything I hadn't encountered with other clients. Yet, at every meeting, I found myself feeling anxious, and at times it was hard for me to concentrate on what he was saying. Clearly, he did not have the full benefit of my skills. While mentally searching for the reason why I was distracted, I realized he always came in civilian clothes, but he wore an off-duty weapon at his waist, not uncommon for police personnel. Having identified the source of my anxiety, I asked him if he could not wear the weapon to the agency. He willingly left his weapon somewhere else, and then I was able to devote my full attention to his issues.

To trust and use your feelings: believe that your feelings can help guide you. Ask open-ended questions. Breathe deeply. Relax. Start where the client is. Build on your clients' strengths and support your clients. Focus on your own strengths and on what you do well.

CARE AND FEEDING OF ON-SITE SUPERVISORS

If you are lucky, your on-site supervisor will fulfill two important roles: teach you to become a great social worker, and become the kind of person you can look up to both personally and professionally.

Ideally, your field work supervisor will also be your mentor. A mentor is often thought of as a more experienced person, a wise and loyal advisor. The mentor uses his or her seniority to act as sponsor, host, guide, and example. Ideally, the mentor serves as a role model, and offers guidance, support, and coaching in order to help the student become successful. If you are very fortunate, you will have just such a supervisor. You can also increase the chances of bringing out the best in your on-site supervisor by the way you set the stage for your association.

Make it easy for the supervisor to deal with you. Set an emotional climate in which a supervisor feels comfortable with you and your level of cooperation.

Let the supervisor know you're teachable and humble. One of the best ways to establish this humility is to admit honestly at the beginning that you're feeling anxious and unsure in your new placement. This is not the time to demonstrate your ability to disguise your anxiousness.

Remember that you are undergoing two inherently regressive experiences: being in field work and being in supervision. That is, you will suddenly be thrust into the role of newbie, in which you are automatically unsure of yourself and feel smaller and younger than before. That's part of the course. The fact that you have those feelings means that you fully understand what's happening to you. That's all. Feeling weak, small, incompetent, or uncertain is actually a positive step in the learning process, and those feelings (if honestly faced and dealt with) can help you learn, grow, and work well with others.

You may have been taught to see supervisors as wise and all-knowing. For you to see your supervisor falter or do something that would negatively affect you or your performance may be unthinkable. But guess what? Your supervisors are human and they do make mistakes. Are they big enough to admit they made a mistake? That may depend on two factors: (1) the supervisor's maturity level, ability to self-evaluate, and level of psychological security, and (2) your ability to create an atmosphere in which a supervisor feels comfortable enough to say, "I made a mistake."

"That's not my job," you may say. "It is the job of the supervisor to make me comfortable enough to admit my own mistakes."

You are correct. That is the supervisor's job. However, if you want to make your field placement more pleasant, meaningful, and productive, you will begin to think about the atmosphere you create for everyone around you—clients, staff members, and supervisors alike. A supervisor who feels comfortable with you can then relax and help make

Ask questions to gain knowledge, not to show off to a supervisor or others.

Be a student. Be teachable, no matter how old or experienced you are.

"In the beginner's mind there are many possibilities. In the expert's mind, there are few." Strive to cultivate a beginner's mind so you can keep learning from the situations in which you find yourself.

you feel relaxed, which makes it a circular reaction. When you create that "safe zone" for your supervisor, you will be more likely to receive emotional safety in return.

Field work faculty have years of experience. They are an important resource.

We have all heard many stories about students in tears after supervision, about supervisors not available to supervise, and about supervisors leaving mid-year for an assortment of reasons. As just mentioned, supervisory skills can vary and in some situations the supervisor may have been appointed without his or her willingness. These factors can greatly affect your placement; in these situations get the support of your college field work faculty, for they can guide you.

How do you create an atmosphere of safety for your supervisor? Watch how others behave who have a knack of dealing well with your supervisor. Learn when and how to talk with your supervisor. An old saying reminds us that since we have two ears and only one mouth, we should do more listening than talking. Talking in the context of deep listening is more powerful and more likely to be heard. Learn to "lead into" a topic after a warm small-talk and set the stage with pleasant conversation instead of barging in and requesting something cold. When you're requesting (not demanding) something or need to discuss something difficult, learn the best times to discuss (and not to discuss) uncomfortable subjects.

The not-so-good times to talk with your supervisor:

- just after either of you have had a difficult encounter with a staff member or client
- during or after a tense meeting
- days that are unusually rushed and filled with tension
- whenever you detect signs of stress in your supervisor
- when you see your supervisor preoccupied with a concern or problem
- the end of the work day, when everyone is tired
- just before or after a holiday
- any time when you yourself are tired, angry, hungry, upset, or overly emotional

With that list there never seems to be a good time to meet with your supervisor or so it would seem. Welcome to agency life! Any or all of these things can occur in a given day. Learn to wait. Unless you're truly in an emergency situation, whatever you need to discuss with your supervisor can wait for later. Use your structured supervision time, write down the items you want to discuss, prioritize them. You may not get to everything on your agenda. Giving an issue more time and consideration will likely only help the situation. Make immediate notes so you won't forget what needs to be talked about. When you are angry, it is probably best to wait until you have processed the anger on your own, if you can. You might do this through introspection, calming down, journaling, talking to someone in your support group, walking around the block if need be, or taking other measures to reach greater perspective and insight in your own thinking. Again, your field faculty are resources; if you are unable to process your feeling, seek their assistance. Try to be open to what you hear.

Sometimes, your supervisor may inadvertently give you unclear directions or bad advice. Calling attention to the situation, heckling, or laughing at a supervisor doesn't help. Ideally, the supervisor will realize what happened and will make every effort to correct the situation, and acknowledge the mistake.

A supervisor speaks: I was going to be off for the next few days, and I was unhappy with the progress note the student had written on a client. Since I was not going to be available, I asked a fellow social worker to speak to the student to help her understand what should be in the note and what should not be included. What a major blunder I made as a supervisor! The student did what the other social worker asked, but that person did not have a clear understanding of either the background of the situation or the issues we were working on. As a result, the advice he gave her was directly contradictory to my supervision and what I had discussed for the last several weeks. No wonder the student was confused!

Supervisors vary widely in their availability. Some supervisors are hard to find and have little time to talk, teach, or explain. Others may feel so pressured by various factors in their personal or professional environment that they are unable to give you the time and attention you may want or need.

Supervisors also vary in their ability to teach. You may run into the kind of supervisor who does very little teaching or explaining, and expects you to function on your own and learn from your own mistakes. "Just go out there and wing it, and if you run into problems, come find me and I'll help you out," you might hear. As luck would have it, when you do need that supervisor, he or she may be nowhere to be found, and you are left with a sticky situation that you do not know how to handle on your own. This is a situation that your field facility needs to be apprised of, not after the event but when you find yourself in this situation. Support from others, whether it's a trusted friend, a school mentor, or a support group of your peers, can also be helpful but cannot replace the field director's knowledge of the issue.

To get the most from the time you spend with your supervisor, bring your written agenda to each meeting. Keep the list with you at all times, so when something comes to mind, make a note of it for future reference. At the meeting, you will be able to keep the discussion focused on the issues that are important to you, and you will not walk out of the meeting saying to yourself, "Oh, I forgot to bring up. . . ." This also shows your supervisor that you came prepared for the supervisory session. Everything you do is being evaluated, especially your attitude toward the work. Your professionalism, as a social worker, is developing through this field placement experience and part of that experience lies in your behavior and attitude at meetings.

Over the years, I have been exposed to many supervisors, both good and bad. No matter how experienced supervisors are, they can still make mistakes. What I have learned is that even the poor supervisors have taught me lessons I have incorporated into my own style of working with clients.

MACRO EXPERIENCES

Macro experiences present a different set of issues; we reference the agency or the meeting as the client. In the ideal world of a student's practicum, you should have macro experiences. Agency life covers the three Ps: politics, personalities, and payment. As a student you have a wonderful advantage, you have no history with the agency; you are in essence a blank slate. I watched as my coworker exited a meeting where they were discussing patient safety. You could see the frustration on her face. She was followed shortly by my student who was beaming as if she had just experienced an inspiring moment. When I had an opportunity to speak to my coworker, she reported how each member attending the meeting was interested only in his or her own agenda. During the supervision session that week, my student began discussing the meeting they had both attended. She was impressed with how everyone was focused on the agenda and working together to achieve a positive outcome. Could the truth lie somewhere in the middle?

One of your biggest challenges in the beginning is to know who is in the room and what language are they speaking. If you are fortunate, you will know people from which disciplines, departments, or agencies are in the room. Each group has its own set of values, beliefs, and attitudes. The language or code they speak is called acronyms.

Everywhere you go, there will be acronyms: single room occupancy (SRO), State Operated Care Residence (SOCR), Intensive Case Managers (ICM)—you get the picture, right? You may want to include this as a part of your learning contract.

My student had just attended morning rounds at this hospital. Her notepad was covered with scribbles. She had just encountered her first exposure to the hospital acronyms. She went down her list and I gave her the full name for each. As we completed this task, she began to have a different understanding of the meeting content.

Be aware that you will not necessarily hear all the acronyms in the first meeting you attend, as my student learned. Some agencies use names that are actually cities or streets for their own use, which can be confusing. You would expect the domestic abuse agency and the Midway Center to show up. It takes time to learn who the players are and what they represent; be patient.

A Frustrated Student

This was a meeting of volunteers for an agency who are expected to work independently in the community. What does this dialogue tell you about the expectations the student has of these volunteers? What do you think his supervisor should do to help him?

NOTES

NOTES

CHAPTER 4

Staying the Course—Routines

A large part of being successful in a field placement has to do with settling in for the long haul and getting comfortable with the day-to-day routines of your agency. In truth, you will probably never get as comfortable as the social workers employed at your agency for several reasons: you're being evaluated by at least two persons—your supervisor and the individual responsible for field work from your college or university. You may feel somewhat under scrutiny during your entire placement. You're walking in as the new kid on the block, and for a while at least, all eyes will be on you. Once you seem to be fitting in, things will relax a bit, you'll feel more comfortable, and everything will settle down to something like a routine. It may seem that just as you're getting the hang of everything, your placement will be finished, and you'll be on to the next chapter in your life.

TEAM AND AGENCY AS SYSTEMS

In the classroom you have defined and discussed micro, mezzo, and macro theories of practice. You are now experiencing all three at the same time and you may not fully realize the process until it is pointed out to you. Any agency where you are assigned to do your placement is a system, and system issues will be present. Large institutions may make it easier to see the system issues on all three levels: departments, wards, and specialty units within the institution. A classic example would be a general hospital, but social work placements are made in small agencies as well. It may be harder to see the system issues from all three levels but they are there. Become aware of the three levels within your agency; they are the tools of understanding why things change and why they do not change. Listen intently at team meetings or department meetings; learn the issues and identify the problems. Remember there are many combinations, so be alert. Here are some possibilities: there is the team, often multidiscipline; the client group; the social work department; the agency as a part of a larger organization; and there is you, your supervisor, and your clients. As a final comment, funding sources are also part of the system; do not ignore them.

One tool that may help you get started, if you are called upon to identify the micro, mezzo, and macro systems in your placement, is drawing an ecosystem. By placing yourself, your client, or your agency in the center, you can identify the surrounding elements and their impact on the core figure in the center of the drawing.

MULTICULTURAL INTERVIEW AND CULTURE COMPETENCE

Before you engage the client in your first interview or in an assessment process, you need to have a solid understanding of cultural diversity. Your experiences will expose you to different cultures. Many agencies involve the staff in cultural diversity training, which is not to be used for work with clients, but for working with diverse cultural groups among the staff. They aim to increase awareness, sensitivity, and understanding among workers that people from different cultures may not interpret a situation in the same way. This is not the same as your classroom discussion about understanding cultural diversity and the multicultural interview. You must be aware that the clients you will be helping can and will come from a varied range of cultures. Your sensitivity to this cultural difference is essential in the helping process. You do not want to make interventions that are inappropriate and useless for these individuals because you did not take the time to understand the client's culture. Yes, it is true that clients are very forgiving if you make a mistake and will give you a second chance; but that does not excuse you the second time and really not even the first time if you did your homework.

Always begin with the basics; treat your client as an individual, respectfully and with dignity. Do not assume you understand a culture because you have read material on that culture. Within cultures, there are wide ranges of diversity. Look at your own culture and see the diversity and similarities you experience with others of the same culture, in terms of behaviors, traditions, values, and attitudes.

- Take time to understand the client's culture.
- Ask the client about his or her culture when appropriate.
- Ask your supervisor about agency experience with specific cultures.
- Find reading material relevant to clients' ethnicity.
- Learn cultural taboos.
- Learn cultural behaviors.
- Be aware there is verbal as well as nonverbal communication.

There are enough pitfalls in building a trusting relationship with a client; these are avoidable if you take the time to do your homework.

A few years back, you did not hear as much talk about competencies required doing your job as a social worker. But for many reasons this requirement has risen to a heightened awareness. This issue is very broad and covers a wide range of areas in which workers must demonstrate competency, including gender, culture, spirituality, sexual preference, marital status, and age, for example, whether the client is a child, an adolescent, or elderly. The expectation is not that you are an expert in one or more areas, or that you have read everything you can find on a population group. The expectation involves you being aware of your strengths and areas of limited knowledge; you must approach situations prepared to learn; be open to different behaviors and different ways of looking at the same issue. If you have never read about ethnocentrism, now is a good time. Basically, *ethnocentrism* means you assess the world and those in it based on your own culture. Your culture becomes the standard to judge others. When this happens, you can easily misread your client's actions and decisions. Therefore, two equally important items jump out. One, you must maintain a nonjudgmental attitude (easier said than done) and, two, you must learn to ask your clients about their culture to help you understand their actions and decisions. Just reading about a culture is not enough. There is too much variation from person to person and region to region and among mixed cultures and transplanted cultures to new lands to expect any one source to have sufficient information.

Some agencies have gone as far as creating cultural assessment forms with prompts to ask certain questions. Whether you use a standardized form or your own unstructured questions, the end result will be the same if you understand the importance of the individual's background.

Recently, a professional I know was talking about a lesbian couple he had met. During the discussion of where they lived, how many children they had, and what they did for a living came this question: Which one was more like the man and which one was more the woman? If you get it, hurray for you, pat yourself on the back. The person asking that question was married and in a heterosexual relationship and he was judging this couple by his standards.

I hope this simple example helps you grasp this important issue and makes you less likely to fall victim to the effects of ethnocentrism.

ASSESSMENTS

Assessments are critical tools in social work, and your understanding of them is important. There are many types of assessments—all with the same intent—to gather information on your clients. The range is enormous, from developmental history, mental status, family history, vocational history to medical history, just to name a few. These assessments are known by many different names, often depending on the agency where you are. So the first order of business is to get familiar with the assessments your placement uses. Ask for copies of blank forms so you can review and look for areas you don't fully understand. You can then discuss these with your supervisor.

Perhaps one of the best ways you can serve your client is to be generally familiar with the bio-psychosocial model of assessment or comprehensive client history. Look for strengths and areas in your clients that need improvement.

Use this information to build your assessment. Some agencies will be very narrow in their focus; others will not be, so follow the lead of your placement.

Remember a strength—large family system or overly involved family—can also be a problem area.

The mental status assessment I learned in one agency is of little use to me in my current graduate school placement. My new supervisor concentrates on my assessment of the clients' needs, but is not very interested in the clients' moods, for example. I'm glad I learned that particular assessment, even though it's not valuable to me right now. I'm happy I was able to build a broad base of assessment knowledge that may come in handy later on in my career as I become more specialized.

Assessment skills may be in use, even when they don't appear to be.

I was visiting my mother in the hospital following her surgery and in the next bed was a patient who had just received a lung transplant. One of the hospital's social workers came to meet with this patient to discuss and review insurance coverage for post-hospital care. The bulk of the time was spent discussing what benefits the patient was qualified for at this time. This seems narrow in focus, yes, but the role of this social worker was to assist the client to be able to manage financially with life-long medications. That does not mean that at the same time the social worker was not assessing the client in terms of acceptance of the new organ and the life changes the client will be making, the impact on family, or the ability to work.

Assessments can be made in many ways, and the more skilled you become, the less mechanical and obvious will be the process.

I asked a social work student who is in a macro placement how the meeting was. She responded somewhat disappointedly that only the client's problems were discussed and none of his strengths. While the field of social work has embraced a strength-oriented focus, many agencies have not and continue to be problem and disease focused. It is not that the strengths approach of the social work profession ignores the problems, but it uses the client's strengths to better understand how the client negotiates the world.

So let's review:

- Find out what assessment tools your placement uses.
- Make copies and become familiar with them.
- Understand that assessments have many names and functions, depending on the agency.
- Always look for client strengths in doing assessments.
- Be aware that you may be called upon to assess your client for substance abuse, physical or sexual abuse, and dangerousness to self or others. Always look to your supervisor for guidance in this area. If your supervisor is not available, see another professional before your client leaves the agency.

Assessments: Generalist Practice

A word of caution: use the assessments your field placement agency approves. Always ask your supervisor about using any tool that is not part of agency policy.

There are two very basic and useful assessment tools that you have surely learned along the way—a genogram and an eco-map. Kirst-Ashman and Hull (2002) do a nice job of explaining the two concepts in their book, *Understanding Generalist Practice*, as do Johnson and Yanca (1998) in their book *Social Work Practice: A Generalist Approach*. If your placement agency does not have resource books on assessments, look up one that covers many types of assessment: Susan Lukas's (1993) *Where to Start and What to Ask: An Assessment Handbook*; this book is economical to purchase.

Some tools you have learned in class include genograms and eco-maps. These tools can help you see the client in a different manner; try them. A great resource book is *Genograms: Assessment and Intervention* by McGoldrick, Gerson, and Petry (2008). They have a symbol key on the cover of their book for quick reference.

Psychiatric Assessment with Mental Status

It is unlikely you will be called upon to do a psychiatric assessment but I want to mention it. As a tool, you can advocate for your client to the MD in regards to medication issues and other issues the doctor may be addressing with your client. A mental status exam is a snapshot in time of the individual you are working with at this time. Your ability to communicate this snapshot to the doctor will help him or her determine if the client needs to be evaluated. I am giving you an overview of what is included; consult your supervisor for more details.

- How is the client dressed: is it appropriate for the season and situation?
- What is the client's mood?
- What is the client's affect: does his or her affect match the mood and is he or she expressing a full range of expression?
- How is the client's rate of speech: slow, deliberate, or average?
- What is the tone of the client's speech: soft, loud, or average?
- Is the content of the speech appropriate to questions and conversation?
- Are there any symptoms of suicidal thoughts; is there a plan to harm himself or herself?
- Are there any symptoms of homicidal thoughts; is there a plan to harm someone?
- What is the client's ability to process thought content?
- How is the client's perception of situations?
- Are there any illusions or hallucinations?

- How is the client's cognitive ability: is he or she orientated the spheres, time place person?
- How is the client's memory, both recent and remote?

At first you may find these questions difficult to understand. If you are in a placement where psychiatric assessments are done, your supervisor can help you better understand the questions. You can see by the list of questions that these are not the typical social work questions you would be asking. However, an awareness of these questions and how they relate to your client may make you a better advocate on his or her behalf. In addition to these questions, questions regarding past psychiatric history of treatment and any history of drug or alcohol use and abuse are also asked.

A former student called to give us an update on her placement in graduate school. She remarked that her superior was not interested in her ability to do a mental status exam on her current cases, but she found it a valuable tool nonetheless.

Psycho-Social History

As a social work student, you are already familiar with assessing the history of a client from your classroom work. I strongly suggest you role-play asking the questions with a fellow student; rehearsing will only make you better. Since you are already familiar with a psycho-social history, I will not detail the task but focus on several areas often overlooked, that of sexual abuse as a victim or an abuser, high-risk behavior such as sexual activity including HIV status, and substance abuse.

Questions related to abuse and high-risk behavior:

- Has anyone ever touched you in any way that caused you to feel ashamed or uncomfortable?
- Has this happened more than once and/or with more than one person?
- Have you ever been a victim of a violent crime?
- Did you ever witness a violent crime or suicide attempt?
- Do you believe this was a traumatic experience and has it affected your life, your behavior, feelings, or thoughts?
- Have you even spoken to someone professionally in relation to the feeling or thoughts?
- When you first became sexually active; was it consensual?
- At what age did you become sexually active?
- Are you currently sexually active?
- Do you use any form of protective barrier during sexual relations now or have you used any in the past?
- Have you ever been tested for HIV?
- What led you to get tested for HIV?

Questions related to alcohol or drug use and abuse:

- Do you currently use alcohol or illegal substances?
- What is the substance, how frequently do you use it, and what quantity do you use?
- Do you believe you have ever been impaired physically or psychologically due to substance use?
- Have you found you have a problem with this substance, or has someone else ever suggested the same?
- Have you ever been in treatment for substance use or abuse, including alcohol?

Assessments, when done properly, are very time consuming, but yield a wealth of information. The assessment questions listed here are only a partial list of assessment questions.

These few questions are just the tip of the iceberg; many agencies have an assessment form you can use for evaluation of substance use and abuse. If not, ask your supervisor to direct you to appropriate material.

Assessment of Dangerousness to Self or Others

Never let a client whom you perceive as dangerous to self or others leave the office until you have spoken to your supervisor or another professional at the agency.

Your safety and the safety of your client is a critical area of practice experience and needs to be understood thoroughly. There are many assessment tools for assessing if your client is a danger to self or others. I review some of the basics to help you begin to develop a frame of reference. Your supervisor is the authority at your placement, and matters that relate to this topic need to be thoroughly discussed with him or her. Some states have laws that address actions you will need to take if an individual is assessed as dangerous to self or others. In the area of dangerousness to others, the California ruling is often referred to the *Tarasoff* ruling. You can access the *Tarasoff* ruling on the web at several websites.

Some questions to consider:

- The best predictor of behavior is past behavior.
- Is there a history of violent behavior?
- Is there a history of abuse, physical or sexual?
- Is there a history of risky behavior, such as those involving drugs or alcohol?
- Is there a history of unpredictable behavior or impulsiveness?
- Does the client experience paranoia now, such as perceiving you or others as wanting to harm him or her or a threat to him or her? Has the client experienced paranoia in the past?
- Does the person have delusions on hallucinations, special attention to command hallucinations?
- Is there a history of suicide attempts?
- When was the last time the client had this feeling and how long has he or she felt this way?
- Are the means to carry out the suicide act available to the client?

A student came to supervision and began to discuss her session with a depressed female adolescent. During supervision, she revealed that the client had reported feeling suicidal. She had not told any of the staff at the time of the session and now it was days later. Her supervisor was very upset and concerned about the client. The director of the agency contacted the family to have the adolescent evaluated by a psychiatrist.

The repercussions at the agency were swift; the student was left feeling embarrassed and not fully able to understand all that had happened to her.

I spoke to her after the event; I wanted to hear her view of what had happened. At the time she truly felt she was able to assess her client but later understood the importance of outside expert opinion. However, she felt like everyone was watching her and it made for a long practicum.

You need to look at this situation in the largest context you can. Yes, we know she should have spoken to someone before the client left the agency; but what else did we possibly learn?

- When this topic was discussed in class, where was the student?
- What training did the agency provide and was this topic reviewed?
- Can there be any issues related to the culture of either the student or the client?

- Why did it take days for the information to be revealed?
- Did the college or university provide a field work orientation and was this topic on the agenda?

It is easy to blame the student, but you need to look at the system issues as well.

Assessing Physical Health

An assessment area often neglected is physical health; some disorders are rooted in physical problems. When it is appropriate, take a medical or physical history; you may be surprised by what you find. Remember that different cultural groups have varying views on routine examinations, such as pap smears and breast examinations. There are two different areas of concern: one, general health and health care, and, two, chronic long-term health care needs. Your client may fall into both categories.

Let's start with general health and health care. Your agency may do a complete physical history intake; if so, take time to read it over. If you do not have that luxury, here are some simple questions you can ask:

- How is your health?
- Have you experienced any change recently?
- How often do you see your doctor (assuming the client has one and has health coverage)?
- Do you smoke, drink alcohol, and/or use illegal drugs?
- If you use drugs, are any of them taken intravenously?

These questions may look familiar; of course they were on your health form the last time you had a physical.

Some questions you may not think to ask include:

- Do you take any over-the-counter medications?
- Have you been hospitalized; If yes, for what reason?
- Do any issues of your physical health interfere with your daily functioning?

The second area that I mentioned is chronic disease or conditions. Here are the related questions:

- Do you have any chronic condition?
- Do you take medication for this condition?
- Is the medication effective?
- Does your condition interfere with your daily functioning?

Chronic conditions can affect your client's mental health; chronic conditions can be misunderstood by other people, impacting others' ability to be supportive and empathetic. Pain is an excellent example of this issue. Now recognized as important, nursing has added pain assessment to vital signs along with blood pressure and temperature. Oversight agencies have made pain management an area they address at their site visits.

Assessing Spirituality

Spirituality is now being recognized as an important aspect of an individual's being. We have known for years that individuals who attend organized religious services show a lower mortality rate and reduced episodes of depression and anxiety. However, spirituality should not be confused with religion; they are not the same. It is important to understand your client's religion and how behaviors, values, and attitudes may be associated with this identity. You will also see that when persons of the same religion get together, they use the word *we*, which identifies them as a group with common experiences.

Spirituality is more a state of mind and will not generate the *we* word in discussion; it is an inner state of your client that can be an important influence and driving force.

Ask your clients about their religion and their experiences within their religious community, including important rites of passage. Ask them about their current religious participation and how they see themselves now. Try to get a sense of their spiritual capacity. Being a member of any of the many religious groups does not make a person spiritual. For many individuals, having a sense of a higher power gives them comfort in difficult times and is a strength.

You want to develop a well-rounded picture or view of the individual. Perhaps, think of it as a picture in a coloring book. You have the outline of the figure and you will need to fill in the colors to bring the figure to a more complete image. What I am asking you to do is get a picture that captures the mental, physical, social, and spiritual aspects of the individual. Optimize the complete picture using the tools of assessments.

NOTES

_____
_____
_____
_____
_____
_____
_____
_____
_____
_____
_____
_____
_____
_____
_____
_____
_____
_____
_____
_____
_____
_____
_____
_____
_____
_____
_____
_____
_____
_____
_____
_____
_____
_____
_____

NOTES

_____

_____

_____

_____

_____

_____

_____

_____

_____

_____

_____

_____

_____

_____

_____

_____

_____

_____

_____

_____

_____

_____

_____

_____

_____

_____

_____

_____

_____

_____

_____

CHAPTER 5

Navigating the Hazards

STRESS AND ANXIETY

If you didn't experience tension, stress, and anxiety while beginning a new field placement, you might have underestimated the magnitude of change you were about to experience. It is entirely normal to experience a certain amount of disorientation, confusion, and lack of confidence as you settle in to your practicum. Any new situation is bound to stir up old feelings you didn't remember you had, and in particular, beginning field placement is such an important change for you because this is a big step in preparing for what may be a life-long career. You must successfully pass the test of field placement in order to move to the next level in your preparation.

You may be more stressed than you think. One of the difficulties with stress is the way it can sneak up on you and hit you just when you think you're coping well. If you're in doubt, or just for fun, you might investigate some ways of assessing the level of stress in your life. There is no one way to accurately measure the amount of stress in a person's life. There are many rating scales you can use to measure the amount of stress you are experiencing. I doubt you will find the time to look at them unless your agency placement has used them and they are available to you. The key element here is the fact that you attempt to recognize stressful situations that you are exposed to at the time you are in the agency placement.

This is the time you will need to practice what you have learned. What are your strengths when faced with stressful situations? Are you good at sharing your feelings with others? Are you a person who seeks out professional help? Or are you a person who can identify your strongest coping skills? "What are your client's strengths?" is a common theme in social work practice. Now you need to apply what you have learned.

On top of the usual and expected stresses of beginning a new situation, you may have additional stressors that have an effect on you. You may have family responsibilities or problems, financial concerns, or health challenges, or you may simply have overscheduled your life with too many responsibilities, jobs, classes, or activities. No matter what your personal situation or what life problems you may be struggling with, you will be expected to keep those problems from affecting your work. When you walk through the door to your placement, your supervisor, your coworkers, and your clients all expect you to tend to business and be fully present instead of worrying about other things. When your mind is taken up with personal problems, two things can happen.

First, your mind may distract you so that you don't think things through fully; you may not understand a situation as well as you ordinarily would, and you may not be able to concentrate fully or make good contact with your clients. Your stressed state can cause you to make mistakes you wouldn't normally make.

Second, if you are stressed, you may need to miss work in order to take care of emergency situations or your health. Everyone has a crisis or an emergency occasionally, but it should not become a regular occurrence. Repeatedly missing days because of personal problems could seriously compromise your work, grade, or progress. You need to demonstrate your dependability and maturity in taking care of your life outside your placement; this is part of learning to be a professional. This is where having strong time-management skills can help you stay organized.

If you find yourself with an increasing amount of stress and anxiety, work now to prevent problems later. Take a good look at your calendar to see how you spend your time. Have you overscheduled yourself? What needs to change? What do you need to do differently? Whom do you need to ask for help? What changes do you need to make in your personal routines and habits?

"A stitch in time saves nine," goes an old folk saying. Take care of tiny problems before they grow into big ones. Don't neglect important details.

Staying organized and planning ahead can prevent many problems later. Lay out your schedule in advance. Block in time for yourself and for rest and recreation. Highlight any papers or reports you must complete and give yourself your own personal deadline before the actual deadline to make sure you can meet your obligations with ease. Begin working on major projects far in advance. Pay particular attention to your daily schedule at your placement so you can show up on time for meetings and appointments. If you don't already use a day planner, start now. Make sure your transportation is reliable, and do whatever you need to do in advance in order to ensure that you get to work on time.

Procrastination can become a major source of unnecessary stress. If you've made a habit of putting things off until the last minute and then rushing to complete them, you may find that with your new responsibilities, such a pattern will no longer work for you. If you have a problem with delaying and distracting yourself, start now to change your habits.

If you have had trouble getting yourself to class or work on time, make things easier for yourself. You may want to lay out your clothes for the next day the day before, and make notes to yourself about tasks that need to be completed so you can get where you're going on time. You can make being on time a conscious decision. Make it a priority to establish the habit of being where you are supposed to be on time.

One reason some students experience stress in their field work placement is that working with clients in a particular population may stir up old feelings and memories from the past. These reactions may indicate that you have further work to do in integrating your own life experiences. These are supervisory issues, so one of the first things you must do is report these feelings to your supervisor. He or she will discuss them with you and help you to gain perspective in establishing the appropriate therapeutic distance from your clients. If you become wrapped up in your clients' difficulties, you will not be able to give them the assistance they need.

In the first weeks of her field work, one student wrote:

I find myself thinking about my clients all the time—while I'm driving on the freeway, as I shop for groceries, even when I'm trying to get to sleep. I worry about them, wonder if they're using drugs again, if they're managing to stay out of trouble. I can't continue to live like this with an upset stomach all the time. I'm going to have to talk to my supervisor.

These feelings do not indicate that you are not ready for field placement or that you are unsuited to social work practice. Such difficulties with separating your own life from your clients' are a supervisory issue. Your supervisor has been able to help many students with this same issue, since it is a predictable stage in learning to develop healthy boundaries. In addition to turning to your supervisor, you may want to spend some time in introspection, journaling, or talking to a trusted peer or teacher. In some cases, an inability to separate work from home life may indicate areas in which you have old, unresolved issues. If, despite excellent supervision and peer support, you find you are still having difficulties in this area, you may find further assistance through counseling in order to maintain your balance.

Fortunately, the practice of social work over time gives us the ways and means to understand and deal with our own issues with ever-increasing insight. As you work with clients with various issues, you will be given numerous opportunities to strengthen your boundaries, maintain an appropriate therapeutic distance with your clients, and become a stronger individual.

Even experienced social workers sometimes get so caught up in the needs of their clients that they forget to take the time they need for themselves. This problem is rampant in the helping professions. Those who help others may so identify with them and feel their pain that they get so enmeshed in others' problems and challenges that they are unable to deal with their own issues.

I recall a student working in an after-school program. She became overly involved with one of the students, and despite her supervisor telling her not to, she went to the child's home for dinner and to discuss the parent/child problems. Her inability to see her overinvolvement resulted in boundary issues; she lost her objectivity and was in conflict with her supervisor.

You will hear advice like "don't get overly involved" or "don't take your work home with you," Easily said, but very hard to do. Keep yourself mentally healthy: make sure you get enough play, whether that is shopping, gardening, sleeping late, or renting a movie. Some people call it *taking a mental health day.*

Sharing information is also great for lowering your stress level. Sharing or just venting to a peer can be very soothing to the soul. Spend some time with your classmates and gripe about the workload, the teachers, and your supervisors and laugh a little.

Procrastination can be deadly. You need to stay on top of your work; that means structure your time and get a day planner. Put in time off to go out to dinner or to a friend's home. Scheduling play time will actually help you get more accomplished in the long run.

The higher your anxiety, the harder it is to think on your feet. That's simple, right? The fact remains that thinking about your situation will help, but you need to share the burden of what is happening to you. Let your supervisor or a coworker know you are anxious; this will actually free you and lessen your anxiety because you have talked about it.

What happens when you become anxious? You look for mental structure. You've lived your life in structure and learned in structure even before you started school. You most definitely learned structure in early childhood from your family's eating and sleeping routines, along with the structure of kindergarten and early grade school.

Structure is a great thing. I am not criticizing it in any way. Structure, routines, and rituals make our lives easier and reduce our anxiety as we follow some kind of schedule, irregular though it may be.

For example, you may have a morning ritual that works for you, such as drinking a cup of coffee, reading the morning newspaper, taking a shower, checking email, and so on. Many people report that when their routines are disrupted, they feel flustered, anxious, and out of whack. The disruption creates unpredictability, which is what contributes to our stress.

It is clear that doing the same things in a certain order can be calming. But there is a negative side to order that also needs to be addressed and when combined with excessive anxiety, it is easy to fall into rigid thinking. Rigid thinking does not free you from the anxiety that you want to escape. Rigidity hinders you and you lose the ability to think clearly. As a result, you begin making errors in your sessions with clients and you feel renewed anxiety over what is to be done and what to tell your supervisor. It is a vicious circle.

The more anxious you feel, the more likely it is that you will retreat to a physical or an emotional safe zone from where you can function only by using excuses such as "she didn't understand," or "he's never worked in the field" or total denial, such as, "what is happening has nothing to do with me and my experience here, don't you agree?"

Rigid thinking merely serves the defensive purpose, and that is a defense to lower your level of anxiety and hence feel more in control of yourself. A key concept to remember is that freezing up is not an effective tool to help you, even though it might make you feel better for a short time. Even the acknowledgment that you suspect you have rigid thinking can free you up.

How you manage your stress levels is much more important than your own personal success in your internship. Remember that you serve as a role model, too. You want to be able to teach your clients how to handle the major and minor hassles in their lives. One of the best ways to do that is by example. Your clients will notice how you manage your own life and will learn by your example. This is an example of mirroring the behavior, as you will mirror behaviors of your supervisor.

SOME OLD SCHOOL: TRANSFERENCE AND COUNTER-TRANSFERENCE

I am reminded of the line from the movie *Drum line:* "We are going to do some old school and some new school." Transference and counter-transference were very popular concepts a few years back and you will find these concepts in analytic theory. It is very unlikely you will be in a placement where you are expected to do any form of analytic work, but that does not make these important concepts vanish.

This is an easy topic to discuss when there are good examples; generally it means that someone is caught up in an issue. There are many articles and chapters of textbooks devoted to the topic of transference. To put it simply, transference is something the client is feeling and/or acting on toward you, and counter-transference is what you are feeling and/or acting on toward the client. Note that what you learned in class is the theory of the concepts; the concepts just feel differently when you are there in field work, "standing in the rain." My simple explanations are a gross understating of their meanings. Some examples from process recordings follow:

A Shocked Student

He Said/She Said	Supervisor Comments
W: Looks like you have a lot on your mind.	
C: I just feel a lot of love in this room.	
W: OK. How are things at the residence?	
C:	
W:	
W: Is there anything you want to talk about?	Good question but not the response you expected.
C: Yeah, I have feelings for you.	
W: Feelings for me? (Silence)	

A Student Handles a Situation

He Said/She Said	Supervisor Comments
C: What do you think about what I just said?	
W: You know that I am a social work student and you are the client, right?	Good response.
C: Yeah, but I feel like this love, like you care.	
W: Yeah, ... I care for you but as a social worker and client type situation.	Good.
C: I know but I could no longer hold it inside of me.	Very open with you.
W: Thank you for telling me how you feel.	Well done.

First, let's discuss the intent from the client's viewpoint. The client does not intend that you be a particular person, such as his or her mother or father. The client is not using conscious thoughts in this process and saying to himself or herself, "let me talk to this social worker as if he or she is one of my parents." Basically, transference is how the client interacts with the world and you are now part of his or her world. At this moment in time you represent some person in the client's life and he or she is responding to you as if you are that person. An example would be the client behaving in a certain manner with authority figures. You are an agent of the agency in your student role. So, while you are sitting there thinking how you are here to do good and rid the world of injustice, your client may be perceiving you in a very different way. Your task—and an important skill to learn—is to be yourself and not find yourself responding to your client based on how he or she expects you to respond.

An example of transference would be a client experiencing life situations as often rejecting him or her, perhaps by the tone of his or her voice or by what he or she says. If you don't behave in the same rejecting way, the client may try harder to get you to reject him or her. Your job as a social worker may require you to help clients see what in their manner leads people to reject them, and perhaps they may learn new skills at dealing with the world. Don't assume this task will be easy.

Human beings have long-established patterns of dealing with the world and each of us has perfected our own patterns, as dysfunctional as they may be: this is what we know how to do. Dealing with transference is an excellent example of why social work students have field placements: You cannot learn these skills in a classroom. We can talk about transference only to a point, then when it happens to you in the field; it is like a revelation, a "wow, now I get it!"

Now, let's look at the second part, counter-transference. You may say, "no, not me—I would never do that to a client." Really? We have seen seasoned social workers as well as students dealing with counter-transference issues, and remember that they are a part of doing social work.

At a meeting of social workers and psychologists discussing clients, one of the social workers with 15 years' experience began discussing one of her cases. As the others listened, they could hear a tone of anger in her voice. As she went on and on, she described a woman whom she had seen for many years who was currently asking for a new social worker, a request the social worker supported. As other members of the group asked questions, it became clear the client had always been friendly and happy, and had followed the social worker's recommendations. The client had recently gone to live in another state, a move not supported by the social worker. At the last visit, the social worker described the client as different: "angry and less cooperative." It seemed obvious to the rest of us that the social worker was angry with the client for leaving her and making the move to another state. The social worker very likely had some baggage to deal with—in this case, unresolved abandonment issues.

This is one of the most common and obvious counter-transference issues to see and experience. You must start where the client is. This social worker forgot the golden rule: if she had seen the client's issues, having perhaps failure as an important issue, she would have addressed the client's anger in a different way.

Remember that social work is about the client, not about the social worker. Save your self-righteousness for the locker-room; the client needs you to be professional. Learn from your mistakes and become a better social worker. If you are in a difficult situation and suddenly realize you are caught up in a counter-transference issue, get help. Speak to your supervisor, be sure to do a process recording on the session, and write about it in your journal to explore your own list of unresolved issues. In the case presented, the social worker was so entrenched in her feelings that she still insisted the client be transferred to another social worker. She needed to distance herself from the discussion to do some self-analysis and evaluation.

You may not have the luxury to deal with the situation on your own: you may not have seen the problem developing. You may be unexpectedly confronted with these issues in supervision. In such a situation, you may feel blindsided, hit by something that was there, but you didn't see it because of a blind spot.

Remember that our baggage and unresolved issues often create blind spots in our awareness. You are there to learn; if you knew it all, you would not have this field placement. Counter-transference issues provide social workers (who are in training, fledgling, or highly experienced) with many opportunities for growth if we will examine them and stop resisting or denying them.

Tip: read about transference and counter-transference; get a basic understanding of the theory.

I was out of the office one afternoon when a male student was confronted by his client suggesting he had homosexual feelings toward the student. The student handled the situation well, but nevertheless in the absence of a supervisor, he looked for a colleague to give him guidance and feedback for some unresolved fears. He realized that transference and counter-transference were at work in the situation. The colleague he consulted gave the student an article to read on transference. He did need this information, but what he was really looking for was emotional support, which he didn't get. Learn to be patient and sit with your uncomfortable feelings. Wait until the right time to discuss what happened.

Of course, if your practicum is with families, groups, or an agency, transference and counter-transference never happens and you can breathe a sigh of relief. OK, I was being sarcastic. Yes, it can still occur; but now in a group setting, you can multiply the possible combinations of individual retractions.

THREE COMMON MISTAKES

There are three common mistakes that almost all students make in their field placements. We have given them pet names and stick-figure drawings so past students will always remember: "Drowning in content!" "Got you hook, line, and sinker!" and "The ship sailed without you on it!"

"Drowning in Content!"

Here, we have a common problem of content, content, content, and seemingly going nowhere. There are times when the client is a great talker and will chew your ear off, or a client seems to talk about nothing, but is that so really? This is the drowning part for the student; here you wish you could ask a closed-ended question so there could be a break in the dialogue. Also there are topics that often go nowhere, such as politics and religion. If you are drowning in content, you have to learn to redirect your client to a more useful or productive topic. Help him or her make a point.

"Got You Hook, Line, and Sinker!"

Often, a client will present to you a bogus topic to get you off track or deliberately mislead you. This may be done consciously or unconsciously, but the result is that you have been reeled in. You have been taken in, "buffaloed," or manipulated by the client and you lose your train of thought and original purpose. Another word for the process is *red herring*—an item meant to distract someone and throw him or her off track. Learn to listen to a client introducing a new topic: is it legitimate, or is it bait to reel you in? If it's bait and you bite on it, the original topic is gone.

"The Ship Sailed without You on It!"

This is my all-time favorite; I find this example with every student we have had over the years. In this case, a client presents an important topic in the session (we may have even discussed the topic in supervision), but the student doesn't or can't hear it, perhaps because of a high anxiety level.

UNCOMFORTABLE TOPICS

Topics that make you squirm can come up on the first day you start your placement, or at any time you meet with your client. The client brings up a topic you find difficult to talk about, such as sex (whether to have it or not, how to avoid it), incest, abuse of self, being a victim of rape and violent crimes, death of significant persons, being a victim of child abuse, or abortion. The list goes on and on. Many topics that can spark uncomfortable feelings in your client may be difficult for you as well. Following are examples:

A Surprised Student

He Said/She Said	Student Feelings
W: You have told me a lot about your father's family; now tell me a little about your mother's family.	
C: OK, well, it was kind of painful to live there. My father hit me with a wire.	Visible shift here—he was uncomfortable.
W: How old were you?	
C: Maybe about 5 or 6.	Trauma assessment????
W: Did that happen often?	
C: No, not really. He chased me	
W: Then what happened?	
C: My father left but they came and took my sister to foster care.	

This situation with the student's client was a complete surprise to her. Her questions may not have been open-ended all the time but she hung in there. The main thing here is the client's history: it is important in order to understand. Also, you can never tell where you will be led in the session.

Remember, there are two issues on the table: how the client feels, and how you are feeling. Many students try to ignore their own uncomfortable feelings so clients will drop the issue to avoid these feelings in both themselves and the student. That tactic works well to reduce anxiety in the short term, but of course you realize that if you shut your client down on that topic, you have lost a valuable opportunity to discuss significant issues and make long-term progress. Some clients are persistent and keep presenting the topic again and again in a different way, as if to say, "hello, I have something to say to you." So, the ignoring-it approach will not get you the relief you want. You need to get past your own personal discomfort, because sooner or later you will have to address these issues in your client meetings and with your supervisor.

Oh, how we dread the second! Here is the deal: the client has brought this issue to the table; there can be a dozen reasons for you and your supervisor to ask: why now? It does not matter; you have to deal with it. Use the skills you have at your disposal all the time: the ability to ask questions. Use your natural interest in the client to ask questions about the topic. A simple question like "what made you think of that issue?" or "is that an important issue?" or "can you tell me more?" will help. In some situations, the topic introduced may be the result of an event that occurred to the client recently that triggered the memory and the introduction to the topic.

A client has just come from a health group where the topic was sexually transmitted diseases. The client now begins the meeting with, "I was thinking of joining the Marines, but I am not sure, since I will have to have a lot of sex when I am on leave."

As you learn to be an effective social worker, you will see how important it is for you to be able to deal with sensitive topics within your own experience. As you mature in your abilities, you will become seasoned and find it easier when clients explore difficult subjects.

There is always the issue of trust in the relationship. From the day you start with a client to the last time you are together—be it after six months or two days—you must establish trust with your client. Engagement may be the most important part of working with clients. If you have not established a working relationship built on trust, it is unlikely that your clients will bring up these topics unless they are testing your commitment to them.

Clients will sometimes introduce a difficult topic that is emotionally charged at the end of their time with you. This tactic allows the subject to be presented but not discussed until the next meeting. I call them *door knob* comments, comments made as the client exits the door.

A supervisor speaks:

I was seeing a family of four—mother, father, and two boys who were preteen. I was meeting with the mother who was sharing details of her life premarriage and since. Our time was up and she stood to leave, as she opened the door she said; "sometime we will have to talk about when I was date raped."

What topics would be difficult subjects for you to discuss with your client?

This example demonstrates a powerful and uncomfortable topic that she wanted to talk about. She could not introduce the topic, speak about it, and explore her feeling in one continuous motion. You will experience this at some point in your career.

HELPLESS AND HOPELESS: BAD FEELINGS OR GOOD FEELINGS?

Every social worker at some point in training will likely experience feelings of helplessness and hopelessness. This is a good place to be as a student, though at the moment it may not feel like a good place to be. These feelings are tremendous learning opportunities and at the same time give you insight into the feelings of your clients as well as their family members or significant others.

Let's look at the feelings of helplessness and hopelessness and try to achieve a deeper understanding. As providers of services, we listen to situations in our clients' lives that cause them great discomfort. There is a natural feeling of wanting to do something to help, to lessen their emotional pain, and that entails more than just listening to the client. Often our clients will say to us, "don't just sit there, say something." This statement evokes two concepts that you need to understand.

First, your need to help or do something may be driven simply by your discomfort with the feelings you are experiencing while with this individual. This is a common feeling that happens when you are working with clients. When the client says, "say something," that doesn't mean you are to become his or her rescuer. Rescue mentality and behaviors are driven by your inability to tolerate discomfort. Your client may simply be asking for your empathy, compassion, and understanding.

If you are having these uncomfortable or helpless feelings while dealing with your client, remember that you may not be alone with these feelings. The family members and friends may have the same feelings of helplessness when they are in the presence of your client. This may give you a clue as to why they do not want to have frequent contact with your client. These are not warm and fuzzy feelings, and what people try to do is come up with ideas to help, and at the same time lower the intensity of these feelings inside themselves; that is what you will want to do as well. But you should not, because you should talk to your supervisor before you act.

The key is to understand what you are doing for your client and what you may want to do for yourself. So why is it a good thing to feel these feelings? Because you get an understanding of what others may experience with this client and you can learn to use your feelings as a guide.

Second, interventions for the moment will not last. Clients need to find solutions that they can use when they are not with you, which is most of the time. That seems obvious, but when you are in there with the client, it is much harder to understand and remember. You may feel anxious, fearing that you are not being helpful *enough* to your client.

You may have a hard time finding material to read on helplessness. At times it may get confusing, as to where is the line in the sand that says "now I give suggestions" and "now I just listen." The difference is learned by practice in the field and by trial and error. Remember the difference between errors of technique and errors of the heart. If you made an intervention and it failed or went poorly, you don't make another one without some evaluation of the situation. Try not to make the same mistake twice; clients are very willing to give you a second chance. Watch your feelings and use them as a guide. If you are feeling helpless and hopeless, don't suggest quick fixes.

USING PROPS: TOOLS AND GIMMICKS

It seems like a contradiction that you go into a profession that uses verbal skills, and then you look for props to do your job. There are times and situations that require props, but that is not the general rule. There are times that sitting with your clients and doing genograms with them can really engage them in the moment, and there will be times you will be filling out forms with your clients.

I was sitting in my office one morning doing some paperwork when my social work student arrived for the day. She was carrying a golf putter, golf balls, and a box containing a battery-operated putter cup. I was aware we had a new client in the program who enjoyed golf, so I quickly put it together. She gave a logical explanation of why she thought these props would be useful in establishing rapport with her client.

However, the student had not yet engaged the client in conversation, but made an assumption that this game would be a way to relate to the client. It is likely that she was looking for a way to fill the time with her client. She was lacking the confidence to rely on her verbal skills as a social worker. Remember to look at how you are feeling in the situation. Facing your feelings in such a situation can be difficult. You also need to deal with your feelings about your placement, supervision, and possibly your lack of confidence, but these feelings are essential to your learning.

A student came to me and said she had run out of ideas to help her client and wanted me to give her new suggestions. I asked what she had been working on in the sessions; that's what supervisors ask. This student's response to me was that she had been working on getting the client in a program so he could get a high school diploma. What she failed to do in this situation was to follow the basic tenet: start where your client is! In this case, the client had very low motivation and had difficulty just getting up and dressed in the morning. So the goal of a high school class was not realistic at this time. To work on this goal prematurely will set the client up for failure. The prop in this situation was the student's comfort in making calls to find out how to apply and filling out applications.

This process recording is an example of using pamphlets as props. What you see are the well-planned intentions of the student.

He Said/She Said	Supervisor Comments
C: I sleep a lot, this medication is making me tired.	
W: That is one of the side effects of. . . .	Sense you are avoiding topics. Why talk about medication? Is that within your control?
W: (I reached into my desk draw, where I keep all the information pamphlets.) This doesn't tell a lot about all of the meds, but it does talk about. … (I point out the side effects.) Would you like to keep this book?	Why are you looking for material on his medication?
C: No, thank you.	
W: OK, well if you do want one, there are more in the hallway.	
C: I'm not sure if I am on….	
W: … is for your illness.	

So let's review the topic of using props. First, always start where the client is. Second, always start where the client is! The point being, know what your client's needs are and you will always be moving in a positive direction. Keep a realistic view of what you and your client are working toward: in order to get to C you have to start at A and pass B. A client who wants to start at C may be headed for failure. Your job is to be there for your client. If your client wants to start at C, then whether or not you approve, that is where the client is.

NOTES

NOTES

CHAPTER **6**

Saying Goodbye

TERMINATION

Ending is a complex subject. You are not just terminating with the agency and clients. You are also terminating with the staff at your placement, your college or university if you are a senior or a second-year grad student, your fellow students, and the lifestyle of a student. This is a huge task that cannot be taken lightly, but is often underestimated. Some roles you play will last your entire lifetime; other roles, such as being a student, will come to an end. Your role at your placement will also come to an end. I will later discuss termination with clients, but the main focus here is on you the student and your experience with the termination process and transition.

You have experienced the termination process many times in your life; this is not new but what is different is your direct focus on the process and conscious awareness. If you stop to think about it, termination, transitioning, and loss are all bundled up together here. Your experience in this arena began way back in grade school. Remember when you won that goldfish, by bouncing a ping pong ball into a jar. Yes, the fish lived a week or two before it died—your first experience with loss and termination. Need I go on with the list of other pets, such as hamsters, mice, dogs, and cats? Then there was the time you had to change schools or move to a new town or state. Somewhere along the way some relative died and your family carried out the tradition of their culture. The point I am making here is that you have a vast amount of experience in this area. However, you have never been in this situation: a social work student in a practicum and it is ending. Many of these old feelings may resurface at this time, so be aware!

VOLUNTEERISM

A common phrase I hear students tell me is, "I plan to come back after the semester ends and be a volunteer." That is not termination. Termination is ending and separating; saying you are coming back as a volunteer implies you will not have to take termination seriously. And I must tell you I have never seen anyone go back as a volunteer, but my experience in this area is limited. Some do think that volunteering can be a stepping stone to employment and resume building. You know my view on the subject.

I tried this mental trick once when my mother passed away after six months in a nursing home. I had helped her at dinner time, five to six days a week. I knew all the staff by first name and many of the other residents. And yes, I said I would be back as a volunteer.

PREPARING FOR THE TRANSITION

Termination can evoke many feelings in you and the persons around you, staff and clients. Termination is coming from all directions at the same time with varying levels of intensity. No one can make the process less intense, but you can learn coping skills to deal with the changes and maximize the learning as you close out your field placement. Let's talk about how prepared you are for this transition. Oh yes, as much as your exit is emotionally rich, your new beginnings, whether a job search, graduate school, or something else, bring with them new anxieties, stressors, and change. So how prepared are you? Some things you need to consider are listed below.

- Have you shared your feelings and concerns with friends and/or family?
- Who in your life can be a support at this time?
- How well have you managed changes in your life up to this point?
- Can you identify your thoughts, feelings, and concerns?
- Do you recognize the importance of staying healthy (adequate rest and nourishment)?
- Have you made a to-do list?

Endings can be an opportunity to reflect on the progress you have made in becoming a professional social worker. It is also a time to assess the progress your clients have made during their association with you.

- Are you leaving unfinished work, such as being part of a committee working on a new agency policy?
- Are you leaving clients in the midst of a crisis?
- Are there persons you cannot locate to say good-bye?

Above all, termination is an evaluation period of your work. This is a real opportunity to reflect on your experience and self-evaluate your work as a professional social worker.

If you have not taken our advice to write in a journal over the course of the year, it is not too late. Writing may help you organize and understand the feelings you experience at this time.

TERMINATION: "YOURS"

This is an important step; often, it is not fully understood, perhaps because of the strong emotional component involved. In their book, *The Practicum Companion for Social Work*, Berg-Werger and Birkenmaier have put together a helpful list of questions social workers can ask themselves; it is well worth the time. Often, in the social work department office, you will find a small library of textbooks; see if your department office has this book. This is a time when students often become reflective on their social work practicum and this will not be the last time you become reflective.

Students ask themselves:

- What have I learned this year?
- What skills do I have?
- What are my strengths and areas yet to be developed?
- As a social worker, am I good enough?
- Do I like what I am doing?
- Is there a place for me in the field? What is my niche?
- What are my social work interests at this time (setting and population)?

These are important questions that you will need to address, but first you need to exit the practicum. Focusing on these questions is a distraction from the work that you need to do. Often, because of the intensity of placement work and the enormous amount to time and emotional energy that goes into a placement, we can't see the forest for the trees. Look for supports to help guide you. Your class would have been discussing termination for some time now. What have you learned that is now a resource to you? Your supervisor will be a good source who can explain how termination topics are discussed in that particular agency and the norm for their population. That does not mean you should assume that all terminations are the same or alike. What is important to learn is the process of termination. The termination procedure in your placement may differ from the procedure in other agencies.

Questions to ask your supervisor

- What is the agency's policy on termination?
- What time frame does your supervisor suggest?
- Does your supervisor know that you are discussing termination in class?
- Have you and your supervisor set a date to start the termination process?
- What warnings or pitfalls has your supervisor mentioned?
- Have you discussed with your supervisor when to start termination with the agency staff?
- When will you and your supervisor start the termination process or has it already begun?

This may be a good place to introduce you to the concept of *mirror-mirror*. Mirror-mirror is what happens to you in your placement in supervision and is also happening to your client at the next level. You may not see this clearly till the placement is over and you have moved on to new things. Or you may come face to face with this process during the end stages of your placement. Whenever it happens, it is a time for you to learn at a different level than you have till this point in time. I do not wish to sound vague or philosophical; but like the concepts of transference and counter-transference, you need to experience the process to fully understand. So what is mirror-mirror?

MIRROR-MIRROR

This topic could have been placed anywhere in the book, but I choose to present it here because you will have the greatest opportunity to understand this experience while you are reflecting on your placement.

Your experiences with your supervisor are often a reflection of the work you are doing with clients assigned to you. So as you prepare to terminate with your clients, your supervisor is preparing to terminate with you. As you have been reflective with your clients and reviewed their progress, so too will your supervisor be reflective with you. You have looked at the notes you have taken on your clients, the process recordings, and any contracts or goals that you and your client agreed to work toward. You have reflected on the progress of your family meetings or the committee you co-chair. You have a learning contract that you set out to meet that was agreed upon by you and your supervisor. You have goals set for your group or committee. Here is an opportunity to reflect on your progress in your placement. Do not be surprised if you find that you have quickly met some of your goals, some never got addressed beyond doing the learning contract, and there were other learning goals that you experienced and never knew you had. This experience may be very similar to the experiences of your clients, families, or organizations. This is an example of the mirror-mirror concept I have been speaking about in this section. Termination is the best time to highlight this topic. You have grown as a professional social worker and at this time you are in the best position to understand this event.

Once again, this is part of becoming a professional social worker. The more time you are exposed to the field in your placement and in your future work, the more you will begin to recognize this concept. So what is mirror-mirror exactly? Well, I can call it a parallel process or parallel processes. You can think of it as being in a fish bowl with your client, and your supervisor and the agency as the next level of fish bowl—a fish bowl in a fish bowl. Or you can see the process as simply a reflection or whatever way you can best conceptualize. This process is not as important as your understanding of the concept.

STUDENT POWER

Here are just a few questions to get you started on thinking about your placement and the role you played. Often, social work students feel powerless and do not recognize the impact they have with their clients and on the agency as well. Students do have an effect on the agency where they do their placement and perhaps on their college. Students placed at the agency where I supervise students are asked to do an organizational change project as part of their social work curriculum, and several of those projects have been used over time.

For example, one student suggested we have an educational/health component in the agency. She approached the nurse who then ran a health group, and was able to effect change in the agency that lasts to this day. It was a small action that reaped big rewards. Many of our clients do not eat breakfast; so she introduced the idea of a fruit bowl to be placed near the sign-in sheet. Sounds simple? Yes; but the gains were great. One student developed a community resource booklet for the women's shelter. A third student created a phone directory of clients of the Office on Aging.

My personal favorite was the student who worked on a committee that created a new hospital-wide policy on patient care. After one of the meetings, a list of changes was released for review. The student was surprised and delighted that a number of her suggestions and revisions were included.

These student experiences are not unique and happen often in small ways. I include this information to show you that as you depart, you can know that you have had an impact on the agency. It can make leaving harder, or the reverse; it's all in your perception.

CLIENT TERMINATION

Termination with clients can occur at any time while you are in your placement. Termination can occur for various reasons during the course of your placement. Agency life is not neat. It is not organized so that clients terminate with you the same time you terminate from the agency. Some of the clients assigned to you may move on long before your time is up. Others will need to be transferred to other staff at your agency. Their treatments or goals may not be completed; however, you still will need to terminate with your clients. For example, if you are working with a group or committee, they may not have an end date. Their sessions can be ongoing with no target date to end. On the other end of the spectrum, you may be working with clients who have short-term goals and you could be experiencing rapid turnover. A shelter for the homeless could have different clients and some the same; a shelter for battered individuals could be for short-term stays; and a nursing home could have residents who are there long after you are gone.

Termination is a bridge that many of us would rather not take because it is often filled with unpleasant feelings. Some terminations will not bring with them strong feelings, but others will. The level of feelings evoked will depend on the nature of the time you spent with your clients and your level of engagement with them, how much in touch you are with your feelings, and your past experiences with termination.

You must understand that termination may occur on many levels, so you need to stay alert to experience whatever is happening to you emotionally. There will be distraction at the end of the term finals, and if you are a senior, you will have graduation to think about. There is a great deal to learn in the termination phase, so stay focused.

There are books written on the subject of termination—how to do it correctly and what it means to your client. In the end, you still have to say good-bye when you leave.

You may say that you would like to avoid termination by just going silently into the night. But guess what? You just did one type of termination. And after an extended time doing a practicum, you do have feelings about your clients and the people you spend the day with at the agency.

Here are some samples of process recordings dealing with termination. These are real-life examples only, and should not be mistaken as the only or ideal way to terminate.

The following discussion is about a student's meeting with a client, about three weeks before the termination, meaning they may have about three more sessions together at most.

Clients are often experts at termination, having over the years had many social workers come and go. But were these terminations positive experiences, the type that you hope will help your client grow in relationships?

A Student Begins Termination

He Said/She Said	Supervisor's Comments
W: I've told you that I will be leaving at the beginning of May. (Remind him and prepare for our termination. I have to think of how I'm going to terminate.)	I know termination is being discussed in class but we have not discussed it. Feels like "Don't get too close—I am leaving."
C: Yeah, you're gonna make a great social worker.	
W: Thank you.	I think you just terminated with the client.
C: Who can I talk to when you're gone?	
W: Well, that's something I've been thinking about. You worked with . . . first, right?	
C: Yeah, she was nice.	
W: You liked her?	
C: Yeah. (I was relieved.)	

Just because you are discussing termination in class does not mean it is time to start termination in your practicum. As mentioned before, get to know the standard in your agency. Some shorter time frame. There are no strict rules for this and you need to follow the policies of your agency, not your classroom discussion or some author you read in class. If you find yourself in conflict, then you must put the issue on the table for discussion with both your field supervisor and the director of field work at your college or university.

Be aware of your motivations; you're anxious to finish college and your practicum. You are anxious to complete this final phase before you forget the material so you can focus on the papers you have left until the last few weeks. The closer you get to the end of the year, the harder it can be to concentrate. You need to be aware of what you are feeling and how those feelings affect your work. If you are fortunate and have a good supervisor, he or she will help you stay focused on the topic of termination and separation from the agency. As stated before, be aware of your feelings in each session with your client. This is a valued tool for the client–social worker process.

Have clients expressed concern about who will help them when you are gone? The student had been thinking about this and was ready with an answer. In this case, she knew the agency policy was that clients who were assigned to students returned to their prior social worker. But what if she had not discussed the transfer with the previous social worker or with her supervisor? You can see the importance of having discussed this with your supervisor before the topic is discussed openly and before commitments are made.

Remember the rule, discussed in Chapter 2: always be honest and truthful to your clients. Here the student was very honest, but there was another issue not being addressed. J said he liked ML, but *don't assume*. The student assumed the client meant that ML was a good person to talk to about his issues, or did it mean something else? It might mean that he was romantically attracted to her. It is better to explore and ask than to assume.

In this case, starting termination met the need of the student, as she was anxious to start termination and reassure her client he would be seen. His liking of ML reassured the student. So here you can see there are several issues happening at the same time. The student was discussing termination in class and was eager to start the process.

The student wanted to assure the future of her client, of whom she was now feeling protective after a school year together. Simply put, she wanted to do a good job. I hope this very simple example helps you see some of the complexity of termination work.

There are no set rules as to how to terminate with a client. There are guides and each agency has its own views on the topic, as there are different views among workers at the agency. At many agencies, the client population has experienced more terminations than you have. Clients have seen social workers, psychiatrists, case managers, intake workers, and assorted other professionals and paraprofessionals come and go. The clients may be very connected to the agency or institution. These kinds of clients have a wealth of experiences with both good and bad terminations with staff. But notice I said these clients are connected to the agency, not to particular individuals. Do you understand this concept?

This next process recording was close to the time the student would be ending with the client; it demonstrates there is work until the very end.

Client has unfinished business

Students often worry about being good students and always doing the right thing, whether for the client or for their supervisor.

He Said/She Said	Student's Feelings
C: . . . I haven't seen my child in 5 years. She is 9 now.	She seems very confused today.
W: She's an adult now and you have a grandson.	I will check with her residence to see what her counselor thinks.
C: Yes, I know.	
W: I have not been able to reach her.	Still thinks that her daughter is a small child.
C: No? I want to speak to her. I love my children.	
W: I am trying to find her. But I am leaving in 2 weeks.	
C: You're leaving? Where are you going?	We discussed this last week.
W: . . . will take my place. She will meet with you.	
C: I will miss you.	
W: Thank you, I will miss you,. . . . . . .will take good care of you.	I feel I really made a connection with her.
C: Yes, thank you, can I go now?	I wonder if she is avoiding the termination topic here.

As you can see, this termination was different, but still there were issues. I want to point out that we tend to block out topics that are unpleasant to us, like termination. So I tell my students, "don't be surprised when a client says you never told me you were leaving!" With that point in mind remember this: don't discuss termination during the fourth week before the end and then not mention it the next time you are with the client. I realize you too might like to avoid the topic, but your job is to help the client deal with your leaving.

In this example, the client talking about the loss of the children and wanting to see them indicates that the student must have spoken about leaving in an earlier session.

Many times the topic of termination will come in a discussion that involves a loss that may seem unrelated at first. As said before, the loss may include anything from a pet cat or dog, aquarium fish, lost objects, or people from the past who are missed. You may not pick this up when face to face with your client or in a group, and you may become aware of the topic only after the fact, but you then can use it in the next meeting with the client. It can be easier to spot this topic in a group, since they are often co-lead so you are not constantly "on." Or, while others in the group address each other, you may have time to spot this topic.

What if you are in a macro placement? Is termination different? Your involvement with the different individuals you are working with can result in termination on many levels.

A student was placed in a large hospital setting. She was assigned to several small committees and one extremely large committee, which included teleconferencing. When she discussed her time at the hospital, she expressed no connection to any of the individuals on the conference calls. She did have connection to various members in the large group, some she was more connected to than others. Her strongest connections were to the small committee members and three staff members with whom she worked closely on various tasks.

This is a great example of how your termination can be different from client to client.

Speak to your supervisor concerning the policy about accepting gifts from clients.

TERMINATION/CLOSURE AFTER THE CLIENT HAS LEFT

There are times when your client will have left and there will not be time to process the termination. There can be many reasons for this to occur in agency life. Clients may move, get or lose jobs, have major life changes, or have other reasons for leaving. At times, clients may say to you that they wish to terminate with you. They may or may not give you a reason. I could make a long list of reasons for this from the client being mandated to a service, to other staff at an agency not letting go of clients for various reasons. Remember not to take it personally when a client decides to terminate with you and/or the agency.

If you can, explore with them the reasons they feel they want to end. It is also an opportunity to discuss the progress of treatment and the benefits of continuing. Too often the clients are overpowered by your status (after all we know what is best, right?) and agree to continue, but in their heart they want to stop. So they cancel appointments, come late, are "no shows," and at some point feel they are not getting anything out of your sessions and quit.

Now you have two tasks, explaining to your supervisor what happened and probably writing a discharge note or summary. This is not a bad thing. You are the student, and you are not expected to know everything, and here is an important learning experience. Once again you need to reflect on your work with the client, looking at the progress and events that led you to this moment. This is very important work; you will not always have a supervisor to guide you. Critical analysis of your work is to be treasured.

Reflective thinking is a critical skill of a professional social worker. Not all social workers are equally skilled at this task and it does require a willingness to explore possibilities that you may have been a contributor to whatever happened. Being a professional means taking ownership even if it is not favorable. I cannot teach you or refer you to a book that will teach you to be reflective in your professional social work practice. But I can tell you that good supervision, supportive peers, and a willingness to be open is the best way to help you develop this important skill.

STAFF AND AGENCY TERMINATION

Your termination from your supervisor involves discussion about how you will end with your clients along with a discussion about your relationship with the staff and agency and your supervisor. But before we get all teary eyed, there is still work to be done. Each client you were working with needs to be discussed so your supervisor is current with any issues. If the cases are to be transferred, you will have a parallel discussion with the person who will continue with the client. In a similar manner, you will need to have the same conversation about any families or groups. You may be fortunate to have a co-facilitator, so transition will be somewhat different. If you have been working with committees and groups, you need to inform your supervisor about the current task or activity. Your supervisor needs to be up-to-date on every activity you have been involved in. It may be helpful to make a list of these activities so you are sure every one gets covered in your meeting about termination. It is similar to going to the doctor. We often say, "Oh, when I get there I need to discuss this issue." Then in the car while going home we say, "Oh, I forgot to mention that issue." We go off into sidebars and tangents, resulting in some of the material getting missed; this is a time-management issue. The final part of this process will be your evaluation. Be an active participant in the process with your supervisor. Be open to hearing your progress in becoming a professional social worker.

Remember that termination affects your supervisor as well as you, the student. A supervisor speaks:

I have to force myself to stay on track with my students as I begin to separate from them and experience the pending feelings. Deep down, I would rather ignore the termination process, and I am sure I could get many students to collude with me. Sad and angry memories can be awakened at these times, along with many other confused, ambivalent, and difficult feelings. This process is happening to the students, to me, and to the entire agency staff. We have all grown close. It's hard to say good-bye.

There is often an opportunity near the end of your practicum when you can say good-bye to staff and in turn they can say good-bye to you. Frequently, there is some type of celebration: cookies and coffee, a luncheon, and a token gift given to you. This is a time when the staff can acknowledge your work and express their feelings about your time with them and the agency.

Be gracious; take this opportunity to say good-bye to staff and your supervisor. Your supervisor and you may have a quiet moment before you depart, but you might not.

FOCUS-GROUP-SUGGESTED LEARNING ELEMENTS

Have you accomplished what your fellow students think are important elements? This list, of what your fellow students think they need to learn, has been compiled from several focus groups comprised of both undergraduate and graduate-level social work students who were in their practicum.

Engagement:
1. Create an atmosphere where the clients can share their concerns and want to return for services. In essence, create an atmosphere of trust.
2. Develop skills at exploring the client's feelings about the referral/recipient role.
3. Reach out to resistant clients.
4. Gather the needed information for a complete assessment.

5. Define the client problem in a mutual relationship. Is it a problem with which the student or agency can be of assistance?
6. Set goals and identify priorities with the client.
7. Adjust priorities and goals as necessary.

Ongoing Work:
1. Keep the assessment process individualized.
2. Make inferences and hypotheses from collected data.
3. Reevaluate, refocus, and redefine goals and priorities.
4. Identify client supports and use them as resources.

Advocacy:
1. Able to advocate on behalf of the client for services and entitlements.

Professionalism:
1. Adopt a manner and style that identifies the student as a professional.
2. Demonstrate the ability to work independently.
3. Able to recognize personal concerns and needs and not allow them to interfere in the relationship with the client.
4. Able to evaluate your work and yourself as a professional through critical thinking.

SELF-ASSESSMENT

Your social work field practicum evaluation will cover many areas; rate yourself on those areas.

- Engaging the client.
- Establishing rapport.
- Showing empathy.
- Good time management.
- Being organized.
- Establishing goals and tasks.
- Showing good communication skills:
  - Written
  - Oral
  - Advocating
- Demonstrating professional behavior.
- Being prepared for supervision.
- Incorporating learning from supervision.
- Understanding and demonstrating ethical behavior.
- Understanding cultural diversity issues of population.
- Understanding social justice issues of clients.

  Demonstrating strengths perspective in:

- Ongoing work with the client
- Having the ability to:
  - Problem solve
  - Develop strategies to address issue
  - Reevaluate

NOTES

_____

_____

_____

_____

_____

_____

_____

_____

_____

_____

_____

_____

_____

_____

_____

_____

_____

_____

_____

_____

_____

_____

_____

_____

_____

_____

_____

_____

_____

_____

_____

NOTES

_____
_____
_____
_____
_____
_____
_____
_____
_____
_____
_____
_____
_____
_____
_____
_____
_____
_____
_____
_____
_____
_____
_____
_____
_____
_____
_____
_____
_____
_____
_____
_____
_____
_____
_____

SUGGESTED READINGS

Berg-Werger, Marla, and Birkenmaier, Julie. *The Practicum Companion for Social Work.* Allyn & Bacon, Boston, MA, 2000.

Garthwait, Cynthia L. *The Social Work Practicum: A Guide and Workbook for Students.* 4th edition. Allyn & Bacon, Boston, MA, 2008.

Hamilton, Gordon. *Theory and Practice of Social Case Work.* 2nd edition. Columbia University Press, NY, 1951.

Hollis, Florence. *Casework: A Psychosocial Therapy.* 2nd edition. Random House, NY, 1972.

Horejsi, Charles R., and Garthwait, Cynthia L. *The Social Work Practicum: A Guide and Workbook for Students.* Allyn & Bacon, Boston, MA, 1999.

Johnson, Louise C., and Yanca, Stephen J. *Social Work Practice: A Generalist Approach.* Allyn & Bacon, Boston, MA, 1998.

Kadushin, Alferd. *The Social Work Interview.* Columbia Press, NY, 1972.

Eagle, Jill Doner, and Kopels, Sandra. *Social Work Records.* 3rd edition. Waveland Press, Inc., Long Grove IL, 2008.

Kirst-Ashman, Karen, and Hull, Jr., Grafton H. **Understanding Generalist Practice**. 3rd edition. Brooks and Cole, Pacific Grove, CA, 2002.

Lukas, Susan. *Where to Start and What To Ask: An Assessment Handbook.* W. W. Norton, New York, NY, 1993.

McGoldrick, Monica, Gerson, Randy, and Petry, Sueli. *Genograms: Assessment and Intervention.* 3rd edition. W. W. Norton, New York, NY, 2008.

Olson, David, DeFrain, John, and Skogrand, Linda. *Marriages & Families: Intimacy, Diversity, and Strengths.* 6th edition. McGraw-Hill, New York, NY, 2008.

Pincus, Allen, and Minahan, Anne. *Social Work Practice: Model and Method.* Peacock Publishers, Itasca, IL, 1973.

Prochaska, James O., Norcross, John C., and Diclemente, Carlo C. *Change for Good: A Revolutionary Six-Stage Program For Overcoming Bad Habits and Moving Your Life Positively Forward.* Avon Books, NY, 1994.

Sands, Roberta G. *Clinical Social Work Practice in Behavioral Mental Health: A Postmodern Approach to Practice with Adults.* Allyn & Bacon, Boston, MA, 2001.

Sevel, Judith, Cummins, Linda, and Madrigal, Cesar. *Social Work Skills Demonstrated.* Allyn & Bacon, Boston, MA, 1999.

Shi, Leiyu, and Singh, Douglas A. *Delivering Health Care in America: A Systems Approach.* 2nd edition. Aspen Publications, Gaithersburg, MD, 2001.

Shulman, Lawrence. *The Skills of Helping Individuals and Groups.* Peacock Publishers, Itasca, IL, 1979.

Slater, Lauren. *Welcome To My Country: A Therapist's Memoir of Madness.* Random House, New York, NY, 1999.

Suggested Websites

www.cswe.org

www.socialworkers.org